THE

CO-OPERATIVE

WAY

The Origins and Progress of the Royal Arsenal and South Suburban
Co-operative Societies

To Alec.

Best wishes,

Ron Roffey

January, 2000

Ron Roffey
Secretary, Royal Arsenal Co-operative Society (1972 - 1985)

Co-operative Wholesale Society Limited, South East Region

First published 1999.

British Library Cataloguing in Publication Data.
A Catalogue record for this book is available from the British Library.

ISBN 085195 256 9

Designed and printed in Great Britain by
The Hackney Press Ltd.
London, England

To Joan

For her support, patience and forbearance

CONTENTS

LIST OF ILLUSTRATIONS

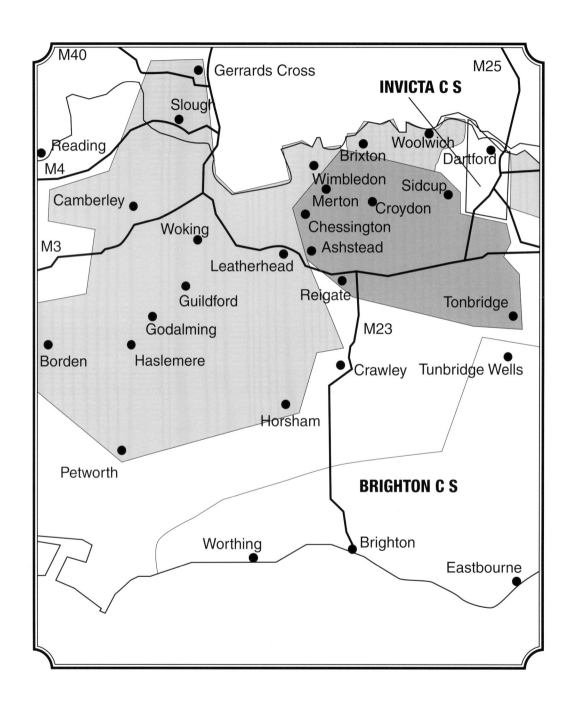

Royal Arsenal Co-operative Society Areas

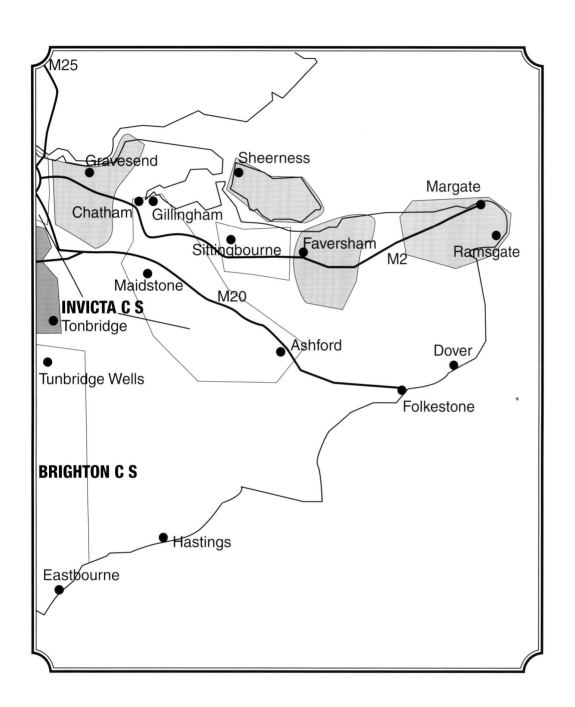

South Suburban Co-operative Society Area

FOREWORD

Ron Roffey has devoted the whole of his adult life to the Co-operative Movement. When he retired in 1990, some of us thought he would change down a gear or two and perhaps spend more time with his grand-children. Not a bit of it! As Honorary Archivist of the South-East Co-op he has kept faith with several generations of co-operative employees and members of the 130 societies listed in this book. By the same token with this massive piece of research he leaves posterity in his debt. Ron Roffey's legendary precision and capacity for taking pains imbue every page of this work, making it an invaluable source for co-operative historians everywhere.

The author does not apologise for omitting the racier aspects of the Movement's fortunes in the South-East, nor does he dwell much on the personalities who left their mark on co-operative endeavour in the region. Ron leaves personal anecdote for the history workshops and the monographs. He has sensibly chosen to stick with the big picture, which has not been adequately covered before now (and has done so before the trail has gone cold), and sheds much light on what is a complex story, providing an authoritative map of the shining network of societies, spreading from London south of the Thames down to the South Coast, which were such a feature of much of this century.

Having been brought up in South Suburbia myself (Bromley, Croydon, Penge, Norwood, Brixton, etc), I found this history particularly fascinating. I recall that the merger discussions which Ron describes in Chapters 11 and 12 began in each case with a lunch: with William Menhenick, then Chief Executive Officer of the South Suburban Society, at the Institute of Directors (of all places!), and later in the case of the RACS, in a small Italian restaurant behind Waterloo Station, with Alan Oberman, then a leading light on the General Committee. As I remember it, I only paid for the second lunch. From such modest beginnings sprang the full blown integration detailed in this book.

It is inconceivable, it seems to me, that any other single volume published anywhere contains comprehensive listings of South Eastern co-operative societies, Committee members and branch addresses, as are featured in the appendices of this book. They are testimony to the Author's rigorous insistence on factual accuracy which underlies the whole work.

I commend *The Co-operative Way* both to the general reader in search of a slice of twentieth century social history and to the co-operative reader seeking to enhance an understanding of the Movement's development in the South East. If ever there was one, this book is an act of devotion by the Author and as such it commands our appreciation and respect.

Graham Melmoth
New Century House, Manchester
January 1999

INTRODUCTION AND ACKNOWLEDGMENTS

On my retirement in 1990, I decided, with the support and co-operation of the CWS and its local Branch Committees in the South East, to set up an Archive to protect the records and artefacts of the former Royal Arsenal and South Suburban Co-operative Societies.

In a very short time it became apparent that there was a need to record for posterity the origins and progress of both societies to the dates of their respective mergers with the CWS. I was aware that the early history of the Royal Arsenal Society had been recorded previously on three occasions. The first marked the Society's coming of age of 1890, and was subsequently updated for distribution to members in 1896 when the annual Co-operative Congress was held in Woolwich. The second brought this early information up-to-date and was published as a Jubilee History in 1918. The third took the form of a short booklet, written by Alfred Dennett and published in the mid 1950s by the Society's Education Committee, which gave me the title to this book.

Background on South Suburban Society was most difficult to find, as little documentation had been retained in the Society's files and no record had been kept of the location of the Society's formal records. However, help was at hand. I was fortunate to receive a copy of an 'Unpublished Origins and History of the South Suburban Society' compiled by Willliam Stewart, the Society's Education Secretary from 1920 to 1947, and written between 1952 and 1954. In view of the paucity of our material, this filled a tremendous void in our records, and I have gratefully used Stewart's research where and when it is appropriate.

Early on I discussed with Stan Newens, MEP for London Central, the joint authorship of a publication embracing co-operation north and south of the Thames, but for one reason or another this project was not pursued. Some years later I was asked by the CWS to complete my research in time to mark the Millennium.

In recounting the co-operative story in South London and neighbouring areas, I have been fortunate to have access to all the above records, which are contained in our Archives, and I have also been able to draw upon material in *Comradeship*, the RACS Education Department publication, *Together*, the RACS staff magazine, and the Annual Report and Statement of Accounts of both societies.

The reader will notice that I have not included my personal opinions or views on the various twists and turns in the fortunes of both societies. I took the view, right at the outset of the project, that I would faithfully record important events in the development of both societies, in order to provide a platform upon which future generations can complete more specialised or definitive studies.

Inevitably in my research I came upon local active members who played significant roles in the progress and development of both societies. In order to record their contribution, I have included brief biographies within the text.

Both the Royal Arsenal and the South Suburban societies were unique in various ways, particularly the Royal Arsenal with its full-time Board, its use of the proportional representation system of voting, direct affiliation to the Labour Party, and continued use of the metal check system for the payment of dividend until the 1960s. In view of this I have attached a number of appendices to provide background to one or two of these features. Amongst these items is a complete list of members who served on the RACS General Committee. This list complements the details of Education Committee members contained in John Attfield's *With Light of Knowledge*, and of Political Purposes Committee members in Rita Rhodes's recently published study of that committee, *An Arsenal for Labour*.

Photographs and illustrations have all been reproduced from our Archive in Woolwich which I hope will graphically support my account of the work and influence that co-operators have had on the social and economic life of the community in 1500 square miles of South East and South West London and parts of Kent, Surrey and Berkshire.

This work was authorised by the CWS and I should like to thank the Society for its continuing support. I should also like to thank Gillian Lonergan at the Co-operative Union Archive for providing information concerning early societies in South London, and to Steve Simmons for diligently reading the material and making sure my punctuation was in order. The manuscript was also read by Roy Martin, Dr Rita Rhodes, and George Warren and I am grateful for the constructive suggestions they have made to the script. All this would not have been possible without the considerable help of Peter Collier in typing the manuscript, completing the map of the area, producing the subject index and proffering general advice. I must lastly mention Steve Sobey and the Hackney Press for design and production work.

Ron Roffey
Spring 1999
Woolwich

CHAPTER 1
SOME EARLY CO-OPERATIVE INITIATIVES IN SOUTH LONDON

Introduction

Some of the earliest records of Co-operation in London are to be found in Robert Owen's journal *The Economist* – published in 1821 at Fleet Street and edited by George Mudie – which Owen made the platform for his belief in the superiority of the co-operative way of life over the competitive way. In the same year, he started the Co-operative and Economical Society in London, a propagandist body to promote his ideas. Owen also helped to form the London Co-operative Society in 1824 with the objective of realising his co-operative ideas.

Societies were formed, struggled and died, the number increasing with the desire of workers to escape from the oppression of the early 19th century.

In 1830, the British Association for Promoting Co-operative Knowledge was formed in London, with William Lovett as Honorary Secretary. One of its objectives was the establishment of Labour Exchanges, through which members could sell their productions to each other. The moderate success of the 'Exchange' established in Hatton Garden led to the setting up in September 1832 of the Co-operative Labour Exchange at Grays Inn Road.

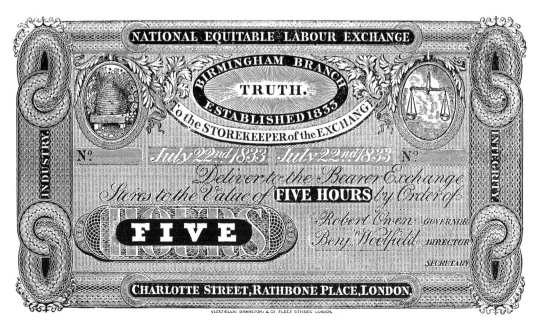

Labour Note

The labour of members was priced at six old pence (2½p) per hour, and articles left for exchange were valued upon a computation of 'hours of work'. Although the experiment was an immediate success with a branch being opened at the Surrey Institute in Blackfriars Road, the exchange failed in 1833.

Co-operative Union records of societies represented at the two Co-operative Congresses reveal that nine were in attendance in April and five in the October. These were all formed between 1827 and 1831 and carried on such diverse manufacturing businesses as tinware, brushes, cabinet goods, shoes, clothing and agriculture. Their funds ranged from just over £1 to £250 and all except two operated small libraries. The First Western Union Society in Oxford Street opened an Exchange in the early part of the year and this was followed in October/November by another opened by the Second Westminster Society in College Street, Westminster.

Of the experiment, Catherine Webb said:

> Though the foundations of faith were securely laid down thus early, the time was not yet for the material success of Co-operation as an economic force mainly because of the absence of legal protection for the funds of societies and the lack of education amongst the workers.

By 1832, a total of 500 societies had been formed but they nearly all failed, a few surviving until the example of the Rochdale plan of dividing surpluses on purchases began to be followed.

Early Experiments in Woolwich

Long before the birth of Robert Owen – the father of Co-operation – a successful attempt was made by shipwrights employed by the Government in the Woolwich Dockyard to establish a co-operative productive society.

Whilst W T Vincent's *Records of Woolwich* contains few details, it would appear that there were many records of trouble arising from the low wages paid to the skilled men in the dockyard coupled with arrears of pay which were often months overdue and this, together with the greed of local millers, who were exploiting local people by the adulteration of flour (the main item of their diet) resulted in the erection of a corn mill in the vicinity of Mill Lane, Woolwich Common.

This initial co-operative effort, starting some time before 1760, ended with the mill being burned down, with suspicion falling upon local millers and bakers who denied the allegations. An interesting account of the incident appeared in an old newspaper dated March, 1760:

> Whereas the mill built by the shipwrights belonging to His Majesty's Dockyard at Woolwich was on Sunday, the 16th instant, consumed by fire; and it having been scandalously and maliciously reported that the bakers belonging to the said town was concerned in setting the same on fire, therefore we,

Thomas Fleet, John Hodginson, Thomas Asslott, George Sargent, George Moore, and Robert Shewing, all of Woolwich, in the County of Kent, bakers, do severally make oath and say that they neither knew nor heard of the same in flames, and that they, nor any of them, did not set the same on fire, or were in any matter whatever accessory to the said accident.

Signed, etc. All six sworn before Thomas Chitty, Lord Mayor of London, March 4th, 1760.

Not to be deterred, the shipwrights re-built the mill and carried on trading for over 80 years.

Woolwich at that time was part of the County of Kent – it did not become a municipal borough linked to the Metropolitan authority of the London County Council (later to become the Greater London Council which was dissolved in 1986) until 1900 – and it is interesting to note from Kentish newspapers of that period that another mill was also operating at Chatham. From this, it would be reasonable to assume that the settled occupation of men in the dockyard towns enabled them to act together for their mutual interest.

Co-operative Corn Mill, Woolwich, 1840

No record of early co-operative ventures would be complete without reference to the formation of the Sheerness & District Economical Society in 1816 during the dark days following Waterloo, when the wages of dockyard labourers ranged from 10s. to 12s. per week, house rents were dear, and illness was as frequent as health. However, work was regular. The most dangerous situation was not strikes – but insanitary conditions and the water supply on the Isle of Sheppey. A malarial fever was an annual occurrence whilst decaying animal and vegetable matter was allowed to remain in streets and roads. It was these conditions, coupled with short measure and high prices charged by local shopkeepers, which caused the dockyard men to join together to supply their everyday needs – wheaten bread and flour and butchers' meat. They also decided to supply themselves with pure water from their own well by the setting up of a Co-operative Waterworks, which continued profitably until 1864 when the local Board of Health commenced piped supplies to all the inhabitants.

Within the Woolwich area, another early attempt at co-operation appeared to be in 1805, when a co-operative butcher's shop operated by

11

dockyard workers carried on business for about six years. In 1814, a Baking Society was formed with profits being divided on shareholding and this operated until 1869 when the business was carried on privately for several years. Later, the Woolwich Baking Society which started in 1842, was successful until about 1860. In 1845, a Co-operative Coal Society with premises in Woolwich High Street was formed and, by 1856, it had over 1,000 members and distributed over 2,200 tons of coal during the year.

Co-operative Water Cart
Sheerness

The 1850s saw a number of societies about which little is known, formed in and around Woolwich. There was a Co-operative Bacon Society in Chapel Street, a Greenacre Society in Plumstead Road and another in Woolwich New Road. In 1847, the New Charlton Economical Society was established at the rear of the Dover Castle public house in the Plumstead Road. It was still operating in 1851, with 264 members and an annual business in bread and flour of £2,250.

In 1851, the Woolwich Co-operative Provident Society was established by Dockyard employees who opened a shop in Albion Road for the sale of groceries and provisions, which successfullly operated until the closing of the Dockyard in 1869. The Society's rules, registered under the Industrial and Provident Societies Act 1852, showed great similarity to those adopted by the Royal Arsenal Society, and it is probable that they were the foundation of those suggested to the first Management Committee of the RACS.

Another Society, the Woolwich and Plumstead Co-operative Society, was formed in 1861 and registered under the Limited Liability Act, with shares of £5 each. By 1862, it had 360 members and capital of £245. Following a bright start, the Society withered away after a year or two.

When it was known that the Woolwich Dockyard was to be closed, a scheme for Co-operative Shipbuilding was outlined in the *Co-operator* for April 1869:

> Government having decided that the national Dockyards of Deptford and Woolwich will no longer be needed for Imperial purposes, it has become a question of great interest whether the men hitherto working under the Crown cannot commence Co-operative shipbuilding. Mr A McLeod, of the Royal Arsenal, thus introduces the subject: 'I enclose you two extracts from the Woolwich Gazette, thinking they might be worth reproducing in the Co-operator and be the means of drawing the attention of Co-operators generally to the scheme viz. of working Woolwich Dockyard on the co-operative

principle. The subject would be well worth the serious consideration of the Co-operative Congress that will meet in May next; and looking at the names of the practical and talented gentlemen comprising the Committee, I cannot but think that some good would result from their deliberations. Also trade societies like the Amalgamated Society of Engineers, with upwards of 30,000 members, the Ironmoulders, the Shipbuilders and other societies in connection with the iron trade, numbering many thousands of members, might turn their attention to the scheme with every likelihood of success. (This proposal that Trades Unions approach changing conditions by using their members' resources and collective strength to take over the running of their businesses is as relevant now as it was then but it still falls on deaf ears.) Of course, there is another important party to consult, viz. the Government. Now, bearing in mind the favourable opinions held on Co-operation by Mr Gladstone, Mr Bright and I may say all the present Ministry, one can come to no other conclusion than that the scheme would be favourably entertained by the Government, if the working men would only take it up in earnest themselves. Besides, it would, in a great measure, compensate for the reductions that are taking place in the Government establishments at the present time.'

The Mr A McLeod referred to in the article was to play a leading role in the setting up and development of the Royal Arsenal Supply Association, later to be known as the Royal Arsenal Co-operative Society (RACS).

There is little doubt that the closing of the Dockyard caused the downfall of several steady societies. This is borne out by the comments of William Rose, the first Secretary of the RACS. Writing from America some years later he outlined the origin of the idea of forming the RACS:

> It was then that I thought that by Co-operation my ideal could be reached, though at that time I knew that none but an enthusiast could expect to make an impression on the people's minds. At that time Co-operation was in disrepute. The old store in Albion Road had closed, the Bakery Society in Greenhill wound up, paying 12 shillings in the pound, and for a year or so there was the shortlived Plumstead Society.

Fickle Londoners

Few would have predicted success in London for distributive co-operation carried out on the successful principles of the Rochdale Society set up in August 1844 by well paid, skilled artisans who were in the main Owenite socialists and flannel weavers. Why should this have been?

13

*Woolwich Co-operative Provision Store
Annual Report, 1851*

Maybe it could be attributed to the peculiarities of the London workmen, for their migratory life meant moving home when fresh jobs were found. Their isolation from family home life – one of the distinguishing features of the Northerner – rendered them less liable to distracting outside influences. The stress and strain of competition was heavier in London, making the immediate success of co-operative trading more difficult. The people of London lacked community life; they were more fickle and thriftless than their compatriots from the North, and there was little chance of them becoming active in spreading the co-operative word where people had lived for years without knowing their next door neighbour. The variety of pleasures and sights which were present in the capital and were within easy reach to form part of the Londoner's life, mitigated against habits which encouraged co-operation.

The Christian Socialists

In addition to these social difficulties, the legislation of the day was not conducive to success. Co-operative societies were legally protected for the first time by the Friendly Societies Act, 1846, though this only allowed them to hold property through trustees. Consequently, they were dependent upon their honesty. A further difficulty arose in that they were permitted to trade only with their membership, whilst small productive societies – those with under 25 members – were denied registration altogether. Therefore each member could pledge the credit of the Society or steal its money without any legal redress.

It was in this climate that a group of London lawyers and clergy who had sympathies with the plight of workers decided to come to their aid. They called themselves the Christian Socialists and produced tracts, poems, novels and propaganda and a weekly journal attacking sweated labour and advocating social reform. They appreciated the need for special legislation and to this end, managed to get the appointment of a House of Commons Committee to consider ways and means of removing obstacles and providing safe investment for middle and working class savings. The case was presented by J M Ludlow, Thomas Hughes, and E Vansittart Neale, three of their number, and by Walter Cooper, of Castle Street Tailors, and Lloyd Jones, the manager of the London Co-operative stores in Charlotte Street. Ludlow and Neale drafted the Bill, and it received Royal Assent in June 1852. The Act allowed for the setting up of societies with limited shareholding and limited interest paid on shares. It provided for regular auditing and inspection of accounts by members, although no provision was made for limited liability nor facilities for federation. This was the first Industrial and Provident Societies Act, 1852.

The Christian Socialists were also responsible for promoting – by propaganda, initiation or the provision of funds – the establishment of the Society for Promoting Working Men's Associations in 1850. Its purpose was to spread the idea of co-operation, and its Central Board assisted in forming, supervising and keeping associations on the right lines. It would appear that there were a number of associations in London carrying on the businesses of bakers, builders, tailors, silk weavers, needlewomen, piano makers, woodcutters and printers.

Charles Kingsley,
Christian Socialist

Few existed for long, whilst others became private profit-making businesses. The reasons given were numerous: jealousy, a lack of unity and purpose, the difficulty in finding a market for their products, the necessity for members to provide their own capital rather than having it given to them, (which may be seen as a means of developing a sense of responsibility towards their own business), and a dearth of co-operative knowledge. Walter Cooper, the manager of Castle Street Tailors summed it up, 'I believe all of us talked too much about rights and thought too little about duties.'

In the same year, 1850, E V Neale supplied capital for the London Co-operative Stores, which started business in Charlotte Street with Lloyd Jones as manager. This became a wholesale warehouse for the Associations and was known as the Central Co-operative Agency, although legally registered as Wooden, Jones, & Co. The agency grew and prospered, but a move to larger and more expensive premises in Oxford Street proved to be its downfall and it was wound up in 1857.

Whilst the Rochdale experiment caught on in Lancashire and Yorkshire during the two decades to 1860, it took a little longer in the South, although the notable exceptions, at Sheerness (1849) and Battersea and Wandsworth (1854), were still successfully trading at the turn of the century.

CHAPTER 2
THE CO-OPERATIVE BREAKTHROUGH IN SOUTH LONDON: 1860 to 1900

The development of co-operatives really took off in the last 40 years of the 19th century and, south of the Thames the retail movement was successfully pioneered by the Royal Arsenal Society and the early societies that later came together to form the South Suburban Society.

ROYAL ARSENAL CO-OPERATIVE SOCIETY

William Rose

Woolwich Pioneers

The Royal Arsenal Society, based at Woolwich in south east London, commenced in a very humble way as the Royal Arsenal Supply Association. It was in the autumn of 1868 that William Rose, born in Warwick Street, Woolwich, in 1843, a member of the Amalgamated Society of Engineers and employed in the tool room of the Shell Foundry in the Woolwich Arsenal, put forward the idea at a branch meeting of the Union, but, as its rules prevented it from being discussed, a further meeting was held at the Lord Raglan public house in Plumstead. At about the same time, and quite by chance, Rose met Alexander McLeod, a native of Burntisland on the Firth of Forth, at an evening class he was attending. McLeod also worked in the Arsenal and, as they journeyed home, Rose mentioned the forthcoming meeting and McLeod said he would like to attend. Thirty people went along to the meeting, where Rose refused the chairmanship but nominated McLeod, who was duly elected. Rose was appointed secretary. Twenty members enrolled on that November evening and £4 11s was collected as subscriptions toward the new venture. They also appointed five managers, Messrs George Bevan – who later was to become Treasurer – Joseph Reed, Henry Mee, T Coles and John Veale.

The second meeting was held in a room in Rose's house at 11 Eleanor Road, Woolwich, when it was agreed to contact the Rochdale Pioneers and the Civil Service Supply Association (CSSA) for advice on rules. By the next meeting, no reply had been received from Rochdale due to the death of its cashier William Cooper, but the CSSA recommended that a start be made with 'honesty and determination' with formal rules to be adopted as and when the necessity arose. Sound advice. However, it was agreed that a start be made with £1 shares, and that each member should have a vote, irrespective of capital held in the Association.

A Start is Made

Business commenced in a workroom in Rose's house, which was used for three hours on Saturday evenings. In two weeks, the capital had increased to £7 4s 6d, and, with this, a chest of tea was bought, followed by 100lbs of sugar and two crocks of butter. The little room was opened for trading on 28th November 1868, when £2 4s 9d was taken and seven new members joined, bringing the total to 27. The business expanded with no expenses being incurred, as the managers gave their services free and no rent was paid for the room.

The first quarterly meeting was held in Burrage Road schoolroom in Plumstead, where a number of rules were adopted. It was at this early date in 1869, following Mr Gladstone's return to Parliament for the Greenwich division, replacing Mr Disraeli as Prime Minister, that Government cutbacks took place, resulting in the closure of the Woolwich Dockyard, and a reduction in staff in the Woolwich Arsenal, which resulted in William Rose being laid off. He decided to emigrate to America to seek his fortune and his position as the Association's Secretary was taken by McLeod. The Association rented 29 Parry Place, Woolwich, on Rose's departure. McLeod and his wife took over as tenants with part of the house being used as trading premises.

RACS Metal Checks

For the first three quarters, the Association's profit was carried forward, but, at the third quarterly meeting, it was decided, amongst other things, to pay interest on share capital and 'to adopt the recognised system of co-operation, namely to pay a bonus on purchases.' The fourth quarterly balance sheet was considered at the December 1869 members' meeting and it was on that occasion that members agreed to a disposition of the profits, which included sixpence in the pound (2½p) dividend on purchases and allocations towards interest on capital, depreciation of stock, which eliminated it from the balance sheet, and the creation of a reserve fund equal to five per cent of the total capital. It was at that time that a blanket club was started and Monday evenings were set aside for the sale of drapery goods.

At the time of the fifth quarterly meeting, the Association was short of capital, and the members were asked to allow their dividends to remain so that the 'Committee might be able to make purchases to greater advantage'. At subsequent meetings, it was decided that 'no goods be allowed to leave the store till paid for' and to pay the committee for their services as shopmen, at the rate of 2½ per cent on sales.

It was not until 17th February 1872, that the Association became known under its new name – The Royal Arsenal Co-operative Society Limited. The Society grew in membership and trade, and six years later McLeod gave up his job in the Arsenal and became the full-time Secretary of the Society. Nearly four years afterwards, he was appointed to the dual office of Secretary and Manager and remained in that position until his death in 1902.

Alexander McLeod

Whilst William Rose was the founder of the Society, Alexander McLeod was, for over 30 years, the builder.

In 1873, the principle of surplus sharing was established, i.e. employees who became members of the Society were entitled to bonus on their wages at the same rate per pound as members received for their dividend, and this entitlement continued until the mid 1980s. It was also in 1873 that the Society decided to support the Co-operative Wholesale Society and joined the Co-operative Union. Four years later, an Education Fund was established.

Expansion

The RACS began to expand rapidly, a bakery was built in Powis Street and deliveries commenced in 1876. Branches were opened in Brewery Road, Erith, Charlton and Herbert Road, a farm was purchased in East Plumstead, a daily delivery of milk started – all in the 1880s. Also during this time, Mrs Mary Lawrenson, of Woolwich, made practical suggestions for the formation of a Womens' Co-operative League, which were subsequently adopted by the Edinburgh Congress in 1883. The League was to become the Women's Co-operative Guild and, later, the Co-operative Women's Guild (CWG).

Erith branch, Avenue Road

Mary Lawrenson, the daughter of a Woolwich printer who published the first RACS balance sheet in 1869, was born in the town in 1850. She married John Lawrenson, a government writer and an RACS auditor in 1876. In addition to founding the CWG, becoming its General Secretary from 1885 to 1889, she pioneered Junior Guilds. Mrs Lawrenson served on the Society's Education Committee for 10 years, the Co-operative Union's Southern Sectional Board and, in 1893, was one of the first women to sit on the Central Board of the Co-operative Union. She died in 1943.

On its 21st birthday, the RACS was the largest society in the southern section of the Co-operative Union and 21st in size out of 1,500 co-operative societies nationwide, with nearly 7,000 members and annual sales of £126,000.

The final ten years of the century were trying for the Society, caused in part by the failure of three building societies in Woolwich creating a run on capital. This was overcome, however, and the importance of Woolwich as a co-operative centre was recognised in 1896 when the annual Co-operative Congress was held in the Baptist Tabernacle in the town.

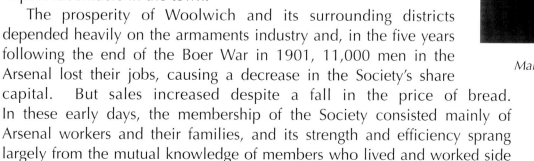

Mary Lawrenson

The prosperity of Woolwich and its surrounding districts depended heavily on the armaments industry and, in the five years following the end of the Boer War in 1901, 11,000 men in the Arsenal lost their jobs, causing a decrease in the Society's share capital. But sales increased despite a fall in the price of bread. In these early days, the membership of the Society consisted mainly of Arsenal workers and their families, and its strength and efficiency sprang largely from the mutual knowledge of members who lived and worked side by side together with their sense of solidarity.

19

Early Days

In contrast to the Royal Arsenal and many other societies, the South Suburban Co-operative Society had no natural home or centre since its activities were not confined to any single town nor to a single county. The society was established in July 1918, by the amalgamation of three relatively small but perfectly sound and solvent societies, Bromley and Crays, Croydon, and Penge and Beckenham.

The Crays Society

It was in 1870 at St Mary Cray, then a busy market village, that the Crays Industrial Co-operative Society was formed, mainly at the instigation of

St Mary Cray branch

employees at the local paper mill, which was the main industry in the district. With its registered office at Anglesea Road, Orpington, business was started in an old cook shop in the High Street, which was transferred four years later to one of several new shops built at the same location. Due to the terms of the renewal of the lease being unacceptable, new shops and a bakery were cquired in 1884, and these were extended and developed five years later to introduce the drapery and tailoring businesses. Deliveries began to be made to Chelsfield, Shoreham and Sidcup, and books and periodicals were obtained from the Guild of Co-operators which formed the nucleus of a library which continued until 1926. The Society operated successfully until 1891, but internal dissensions resulted in initial financial difficulties, which later partially improved, but precluded any future developments which were being pressed for by co-operators living in Orpington. As the Bromley Society was developing rapidly over a widening area, the two societies came together in July 1908, and, at that time, the Crays Society had a membership of 504, annual sales of £11,546, and share capital amounting to £4,933.

The Bromley Society

The first Bromley Society was formed in 1868 as the Bromley and West Kent Society, with a shop in West Street, Bromley, but, due to poor accounting and administration, it only lasted a year. Another was formed in 1882 at the

Bromley Society, Horse and Cart, 1908

home of Mr H D Chard, and William Stewart, in his unpublished Origins and History of the South Suburban Society, records that he was a co-operator of some practical experience in administration, having been the Treasurer of the Penge and Beckenham Society from 1879, a position he held until 1885. Chard was appointed to the same position by the Bromley Society in 1882, and thus enjoyed the unique experience of being Treasurer of two separate societies. An Owenite, and a native of Essex, he was also one of the founders of Bromley Builders (1885-1895), with a registered office at 4 Ravensbourne Road, his private address. The Bromley Society commenced business at 15 Simpsons Road, where two rooms were rented in the basement at 5s per week. After eight weeks, sales were £120, share capital £52, augmented by a loan of £20 from Mr Chard. The net profit was £3 17s 10d and there were 64 members. In addition to taking over the Crays Industrial Society, Bromley took over the Chislehurst Society (formed 1884) in 1892 and the Sevenoaks Society in 1912, which was established in 1897. Prior to the merger in 1918, the Bromley Society had 9,320 members, £65,537 share capital and sales of £217,915.

It was in 1860 that the Croydon Co-operative Industrial Society was established with its headquarters at Market Street. Eight years later larger premises were acquired at 39 Church Street, but, after making good progress for some time, the Society went into voluntary liquidation in March 1874.

The Croydon Society
The Croydon Society which took part in the amalgamation in 1918, was established in 1887 at 85 Chesham Road, South Croydon. However, trading commenced at 118 Church Street, moving to 128-130 in 1888, and extending to 132 during 1897. The Society's early days to the turn of the century were beset by misfortune, due to inefficient, inexperienced

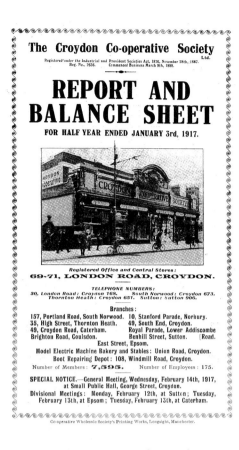

Croydon Society Balance Sheet

management and committees. Furthermore, it was not helped by the disruptive influence of a Co-operative Coal Society which was formed in 1895, with a registered office in Northbrook Road, and carried on business until 1902. The early 1900s saw overlapping problems with neighbouring societies which were to some extent overcome by mergers with the Caterham Society (formed 1876) in 1906, with the Epsom Society (established in 1889) in 1916, and with the Sutton (Surrey) Society (registered in 1893).

During this time, there was also a whole series of changes in senior management but, as in all other organisations, the Society was kept on course by dedicated members. In Croydon's case, there was Charles Bailey, a professional engineer, who joined the Society in 1899 and became President in 1903. He was later to serve as the first President of the South Suburban Society in July, 1918, until his retirement in November 1938 – a total of 35 years in this office. To mark the occasion of his 25th year as President, a portrait by G Spencer Watson, ARA, was commissioned in July 1929 and presented to him by H J May, OBE, JP, Secretary of the International Co-operative Alliance. Bailey was presented with a cheque for £250 on his retirement in 1938 and, four years later, he died at the age of 83 years.

Another stalwart for the Society was Albert Gore, who served on the Board from the 1890s, apart from a break whilst serving on the Croydon Corporation. He also served on the South Suburban Board from July 1918 until his retirement in November 1945.

It was in 1907 that the Society's trading premises moved to 30 London Road, Croydon and, seven years later, to 69-71 London Road, the first stage in the development of number 99, which was to become the registered office of the South Suburban Society.

The first 10 years of the new century saw shops opening at South Norwood and Thornton Heath along with stabling and a bakery in Windmill Hill. The trading operation was further extended by the mergers with Caterham, Epsom and

Sutton Societies previously mentioned.

Mr & Mrs Charles Bailey

The opening of the Crystal Palace on Sydenham Hill in 1854, with its attractions and provision of additional work for the local people, influenced the early societies in Norwood and Penge.

The First Upper Norwood Industrial & Provident Society at Westow Street and the Penge Society in Woodbine Grove, Penge, were both established in 1864. Little is known about either society, except Penge failed in 1868. Norwood, Anerley and Penge were embraced by the Anerley Vale Society which was established in 1868 and ceased in 1872. Trading commenced in Palace Road and, a year later, a store was opened in Woodbine Grove Penge, but once again there is no clue to reveal how or why the society failed.

The Penge and Beckenham Society

It was in May 1879 that the Penge and Beckenham Society commenced business at 4 Green Lane. Progress in Penge was slow and steady. Freehold premises were acquired at 61 Parish Lane in 1882 and a shop opened in the following year. Later on, a library was established there and continued until 1924. An Education Committee was set up in 1883 and, the same year, a branch was opened in Woodbine Grove, but this was as unsuccessful as the previous two ventures at this location.

In the early days, particular attention was paid to social activities and Penge representatives were vocal at most of the conferences held in London. An outdoor demonstration, a new venture, with bands and banners, was held in a field at Maple Road at which Edward Owen Greening was one of the chief speakers.

*Penge & Beckenham Society
Green Lane Branch*

Greening, born in 1836, was an active propagandist for the Co-operative Movement. He took a prominent role in the formation of the Co-operative Union, had a hand in setting up several co-partnership enterprises and helped to form the Co-operative Productive Federation in 1882. Greening started the Agricultural and Horticultural Association in 1867 and took a prominent part in the formation of the International Co-operative Alliance. He was a keen educationalist, supported co-operative activities in sport, the arts and hobbies, initiating the Crystal Palace Festival, and advocated a Co-operative College in his Presidential Address to Congress in 1904. He died in 1923.

The 1880s saw a bakery and stables erected, coal being supplied, and the commencement of the drapery business. A branch was opened in Sydenham Road in 1897 and, four years later, the Society's Central Premises were opened on the corner of Parish Lane and Green Lane.

The Society's territory expanded in 1911 as a result of the merger with Norwood Co-operators Limited and the liquidation of the Brixton Result Society. Further branches were opened in Brixton and West Norwood, but these created boundary and overlapping problems. These difficulties and those associated with World War I, along with the inability, within existing resources, to see the area properly developed, led Penge to the amalgamation with Bromley and Croydon in 1918.

Overlapping

All three societies involved in the formation of the South Suburban Society were concerned with the expansionist policy of the Royal Arsenal Society, especially with its opening of a new bakery at Brixton, well within the territory of the Penge Society, in February 1917. But wartime conditions – shortage of supplies and staff difficulties – were not conducive to them opening a similar operation; they had previously failed to agree to open a federal bakery in 1915 at Elmers End, Beckenham. A committee was formed, including representatives from Royal Arsenal, when it was suggested that one society for South London together with one provincial society be formed but a proposal to table a map with lines of demarcation did not materialise.

However, one thing stood out. Bromley, Croydon and Penge were prepared to lose their identity to a new society but not to an existing society. Thus South Suburban Society was born, with 20,000 members and sales in its first 15 months trading of £770,000.

Before leaving the co-operative retail scene in South London further reference must be made to the activities of co-operators in the Norwood and Brixton areas.

The Norwood Area

Norwood, on the outskirts of Croydon, was described in the March 1940 edition of the *Wheatsheaf* magazine as 'a happy hunting ground for co-operators'. Mention has already been made of the Upper Norwood Society, but, in addition, there was a South Norwood Industrial Co-operative Society formed in the same year, 1864, with a registered address of the 'Jolly Sailor', a public house which stood on the corner of the High Street and Portland Road, South Norwood. For a time, it would seem there was intense activity although the Society was shortlived, failing two years later due to the dishonesty of the storekeeper, together with the Society's failure to obtain suitable redress in the courts on technical grounds.

Lower Norwood was almost entirely a rural district, and co-operative trading was introduced in 1862 when the Norwood United Co-operative and

Industrial Society was registered at 32 High Street. Little is known about the Society except the prospects appeared to be good – so good that the Society opened a butcher's shop – but there is no evidence to show why the Society was dissolved in 1870.

It was not long before another society – The Norwood Equitable – was formed with an address at 'The British Workman', High Street, Lower Norwood (later to become West Norwood). Trading commenced at Auckland Hill in 1874, but the Society's bright prospects were not fulfilled. George Jacob Holyoake represented the society at the 1878 Manchester Congress but this did not help the Society, which had to merge with the Brixton Industrial Society in 1879.

Holyoake (1817 - 1906) had a life-long and generally active association with the Co-operative Movement. He was a moving and eloquent speaker as well as a prolific writer on a variety of subjects besides co-operation. His contacts with the earlier figures of the Movement made him a revered figure in his later years, and as a tribute to his memory the headquarters of the Co-operative Union in Manchester were named after him.

Ben Jones (1848-1947) became manager of the London branch of CWS at the age of 26, having joined the Society seven years earlier. In September 1874, he was honorary secretary to the Southern Sectional Board and, later, held a similar position to the Joint Parliamentary Committee of the Co-operative Union. Jones founded 'The Tenants Co-operative Society', the first co-operative housing society. He was twice Congress President. With A D Acland, he wrote *Working Men Co-operators*, 1883, but more importantly completed *Co-operative Production* in 1894, containing details of almost every form of co-operative productive activity. Jones unsuccessfuly contested Woolwich constituency on at least two occasions in Parliamentary elections.

Eleven years later, a further attempt was made by members of the Brixton Society, living in the Norwood area, to form another society in the district, under the name of

George Jacob Holyoake

Norwood Co-operators, the share capital being transferred from the Brixton Society. Ben Jones served on the Management Committee and was President for several years. By 1906, membership had increased to 3000 and sales to £4,520, but profits were not always good. There were frequent changes in management and, with members' debts nearly equal to two weeks' sales, this was a recipe for disaster. The Society ultimately joined the Penge Society in 1911, after the Royal Arsenal Society had failed to respond to overtures from the CWS to take the Society over in the previous year.

The Brixton Area

Co-operative trading in Brixton began in 1862, when the Brixton Industrial and Provident Co-operative Society was formed with its headquarters in Lyham Road. In five years it had 1,100 members and trade of nearly £24,500 was achieved in six shops. Trading was conducted not only in the traditional grocery business, but also in drapery, footwear and hardware. Shops were opened in Streatham, Balham, and North Brixton and excellent progress was made under the guidance of William Allan, Secretary, and William Ling, who in 1892 was to become auditor. William Allan represented the Society at the 1869 Co-operative Congress held in London and, for the next 20 or so years, the Society's delegates included J M Ludlow, Lloyd Jones, and Mr and Mrs Ben Jones.

The Society probably arranged the first co-operative trip to the sea in 1867, and William Openshaw, Chief Clerk of the London Branch of th CWS, was for a time Chairman of the Education Committee. Amongst his many activities, he edited *The Metropolitan Co-operator* (1876 - 1897), which contained localised pages, confined to the London area, as a forerunner of the *Home Magazine*. G J Holyoake, Judge Hughes and Edward Owen Greening and other national figures took part in lectures, conferences and meetings; and J T W Mitchell, Chairman of the CWS, attended the 'Coming of Age' celebrations at the Congregational Church Brixton Hill in 1883.

There is no explanation for the decline in the Society's membership and trade, although the establishment of a Society in Balham in 1871 did not help the situation. It would appear however that the loss of confidence in the Society was due to the inefficiency of store keepers, the Committee's lack of experience and time in dealing with day to day trading problems, and difficulties in renewing the leases of the North Brixton and Balham shops. These problems in spite of the assistance and close association of many of the Movement's intellectuals in the South of England, resulted in the society going into liquidation in 1902.

The Brixton Result Co-operative Society was set up in 1864 with a registered office in Hope Buildings, Cornwall Road, within sight of one of the last of London's windmills. In spite of being near the premises of the Industrial Society, there was no disagreement between the members of both societies.

No spectacular progress was made, and a report in *Co-operative News* in 1900 said, 'The Society has struggled for 36 years, always meeting its obligations and paying small dividends.' In the 1870s, the Inland Revenue demanded income tax on £200, due to the Society not paying dividend to non members. This was paid on the advice of the Central Board of the Co-operative Union, to avoid the individual members being taxed, and leaving them to appeal to the tax authorities if their income was below the taxable level.

The Society and the CWS audit department successively approached the Croydon Society in 1910 to seek a merger, but it could not see its way clear to come to the rescue. A similar unsuccessful approach was also made to the Royal Arsenal Society. A proposal to liquidate the society failed, due to the notice of meeting being out of order, and this presented the opportunity to the Penge and Beckenham Society to take over the Society.

A review of co-operative endeavour for the 30 years to 1890 would not be complete without mention of other co-operative enterprises which were established in South London by responsible members who were not deterred by the failure of their retail counterparts.

PRODUCTIVE SOCIETIES

Mention has previously been made of the Baking and Coal Societies set up in Woolwich earlier in the 19th century. A number of further productive societies are known to have existed in the south London area at this time. The report of the Co-operative Conference held at Manchester in 1853 lists a Block Printers Industrial Society based on the Nelson Arms at Merton with 69 members, recently registered under the 1852 Act, with no trading results yet available. Also listed is the Atlas Iron Works Company of Emerson Street, Southwark. This society was also established following the new Act, and within the space of a year or so had done £4,500 worth of business.

The handbook to Co-operative Congress, 1896, reveals the existence of the Agricultural and Horticultural Association of Creek Road, Deptford, and Oxford Street, formed in 1867, with trade of £80,000 per annum, and a small engineering company making bicycles and tricycles named General Engineers Ltd of Viceroy Road, Lambeth, which was established in 1894.

In 1873, the East Surrey Bakery Society was formed by the Brixton Industrial, Brixton Result, Balham and South London Societies with the primary objective of making good wholesome bread. The Society exhibited at the Crystal Palace festival in 1888. Whilst sales remained steady during most years of the Society's existence, profits fluctuated with losses recorded after 1890. The Society ceased operations in 1896.

The Bromley Co-operative Builders traded for 10 years until 1895, whilst the People's Society, set up by the CWS in 1885, had five branches by 1896, but eventually went into liquidation three years later. The Norwood Gardeners Society, also formed in 1885, leased land for its 73 plotholders and held flower shows and arranged visits to other co-operative productive enterprises in London until 1912. The Brixton Builders Co-operative Society lasted for 30 years until 1908, whilst the Co-operative Dress and Mantle Makers started in Lorrimore Square, Walworth, in 1889. Two years later, and not too far away in the Old Kent Road, the London Co-operative Leather Manufacturers Society was set up, originating from the Bermondsey branch of the Co-operative Aid Association; and in 1896 boiler makers in Deptford formed the Deptford Perseverance Society.

BALANCE SHEET.

From 31st December, 1855, to 30th June, 1856.

Dr.	£	s.	d.	Cr.	£	s.	d.
To Balance brought forward from last account	110	2	5	By Coals purchased, 863¼ Tons 729 19 6 Less Discount, Half-meterage, &c. 50 15 11	679	3	7
„ Received for Debts and Shares owing on old account	6	15	4	„ Dividends to Members, due at date of last account	6	18	1⅓
„ Received for Small Coals, at date of last account	14	9	0	„ Allowed to Members for payments in advance, ditto	12	10	7½
„ Coals sold, 966 Tons	1034	3	11	Trade expenses—			
„ Entrance Fees (36 Members)	0	18	0	„ Meting 4 4 6			
„ Shares	10	16	9	„ Portering 76 8 1½			
„ Instalments in advance	13	18	2½	„ Trimming 0 16 2			
„ Wharfage	0	7	7	„ Sifting 4 0 6			
				„ Issuing 6 2 3			
				„ Carting 73 7 4½			
				„ Rent of Wharf 32 3 9			
				„ „ Offices 5 17 6			
				„ Hire of Lecture Hall ... 0 8 0			
				„ Committee Expenses...... 2 18 6			
				„ Agent's Commission ... 6 3 6½			
				„ Secretary 8 1 0			
				„ Treasurer 2 0 3½			
				„ Stationery and Account Books 1 9 4½			
				„ Printing Balance Sheets, Check Books, &c., &c, .. 5 17 0			
				„ Postage and Receipt Stamps 0 2 3			
				„ Repairing Sacks 2 1 7			
				„ Incidental Trade Expenses.. 3 8 2½			
				„ Insurance 0 19 6	236	9	5
				„ Trade Utensils	6	15	1
				„ Office Furniture	1	13	4
				„ Shares to 14 Members leaving	3	7	0
				„ Expended in erecting Warehouse, making Fences, Roads, &c., and adapting new Wharf	234	15	9
				„ Balance in Treasurer's hands	9	18	3½
	£1191	**11**	**2½**		**£1191**	**11**	**2½**

PROFIT AND LOSS.

	£	s.	d.		£	s.	d.
Stationery in hand at commencement of account	6	11	3	Coals sold, 966 Tons	1034	3	11
Coals in stock at commencement of account	110	0	0	Coals in stock, 160 Tons, value 148 0 0			
Coals purchased	679	3	7	Less due for last cargo, 172 tons 134 0 4	13	19	8
Trade expenses ...... 236 9 5 Less Stationery, now in hand.. 8 12 3	227	17	2	Entrance Fees	0	18	0
Net profit	25	17	2	Wharfage	0	7	7
	£1049	**9**	**2**		**£1049**	**9**	**2**

LIABILITIES.

	£	s.	d.	ASSETS.	£	s.	d.
1042 Members' Shares	260	10	0	Balance of Cash	9	18	3½
Members paid in advance	13	18	2½	Coals in Stock, value	13	19	8
Dividends not yet applied for	5	3	1	Utensils in Trade	26	15	1
Balance in favour of the Society on last year's account 1 14 10				Office Furniture	6	4	9
Net profit for the 6 months, ending 30th June, 1856 .... 25 17 2				Stationery in hand	8	12	3
Total balance	27	12	0	Good Debts and Shares due on old account, in course of payment	2	4	4
				Balance of Shares on last account, in course payment	4	13	2
				Buildings, Fences, and improvements on new Wharf	234	15	9
	£307	**3**	**3½**		**£307**	**3**	**3½**

We, the undersigned, hereby certify that we have examined the above Balance Sheet, and found the same correct, according to the vouchers produced ; this 1st day of July, 1856.

THOMAS SAMPSON,
ROBERT CARRINGTON, } Auditors.
JOHN CARLESS,

Woolwich Coal Society Balance Sheet. Established 1845

CHAPTER 3
THE CO-OPERATIVE TAKE-OFF IN SOUTH EAST LONDON: 1900 to 1914

Housing Members

The first year of the 20th century saw members of the RACS approve a scheme for the development of a housing estate in East Plumstead to be known as the Bostall Estate. At the outset, the building scheme came about – according to Mr T G Arnold, the Society's Secretary at that time, 'by an over-abundance of funds' – when the Society acquired over 170 acres by purchasing the Bostall Farm and Suffolk Place Estate in 1887 and 1899. The housing scheme proposed the building of 3,500 leasehold houses with the offer of generous mortgage terms to poorer members to enable them to buy their own homes. There were some members who opposed the leasehold principle, but this was not supported by the majority of members who agreed that the Society should retain the freehold in the land. By 1903, over 400 houses

Bostall Estate, Abbey Wood

had been built by the Society's own Works Department, and, apart from a lapse of building for three years from 1909, due to a fall in demand, over 1,000 houses had been sold or let on a weekly tenancy.

Associated with the building of houses, the RACS, in December 1901, was the first society to commence insurance on its own account. Owners of private houses could effect fire cover on their properties at premiums of 1s 6d per cent (7½p) on buildings and 2s per cent (10p) on furniture. The Society continued to offer fire cover on buildings and contents until the 1960s when changes in legislation made it impractical to do so. The Society also acted as agents for various insurance companies, to effect insurance against fire and on life.

Parsons Hill

In 1901, a baptist chapel in Parsons Hill, Woolwich, was bought at public auction to provide premises for the Society's educational institute. This was a far-sighted and courageous step considering the depression hanging over the district due to the unemployment brought about by the ending of the South African War.

The depression however deepened in May 1902, with the death of Alexander McLeod, the Society's Secretary-Manager for the previous 34 years. Perhaps no finer tribute was paid to his memory than that uttered by George Jacob Holyoake who described him as 'a prince among secretaries.' Yet the remark which appeared in *Comradeship's* obituary in June 1902, concerning McLeod's contribution to the Society's development merits attention: 'The Royal Arsenal Co-operative Society, standing like a pillar of cloud or of fire of old, to show to London the road to a better social system, is the monument that commemorates his life work.'

Central Premises

It was unfortunate that McLeod did not see the fruition of his work in Woolwich when the foundation stones for the reconstructed central premises were laid in September 1902. The three storey building, which was built in four sections, was listed by the Department of the Environment in 1989 as a building of special architectural or historical interest; as the listing says, 'The style of the building consciously imitated Harrods of Knightsbridge.'

Laying one of the foundation stones at 147, Powis Street, Woolwich, 1902

The central feature of its 300 foot frontage is a four storey copper domed clock tower, which incorporates the main entrance on the ground floor, above which is a statue of Alexander McLeod, by Alfred Drury of Chelsea; the statue is surmounted by a raised stone reproduction of the Society's seal and motto, 'Each for All, and All for Each'. Within one month of the foundation stone being laid, one half of the new premises opened for business.

Expansion and Mergers

The Woolwich Society, the name by which the RACS was known in those early days, decided to change its tactics in the battle to win London for co-operation. Instead of attacking from within, like its predecessors, with weak forces and weak capital, it decided to conduct the attack from the outskirts – to merge with societies that were well established, and to march inwards.

The East Greenwich Society

In June 1904, RACS members approved a recommendation of the General Committee that the Society merge with the East Greenwich Society. That Society had three shops, one of which it operated, the remaining two being leased, the leases for which expired in the following year. This merger marked the beginning of an era of expansion.

East Greenwich branch

Woolwich and its surrounding districts were changing rapidly from green fields to houses, heavily populated by members of the society. One such area was adjacent to Plumstead Common, on the site of an old pottery and house, which for generations had belonged to the Dawson family. A shop to be known as The Links (after the name of the house) was erected and opened in December, 1904.

It was at that time that the Southern Section of the Co-operative Union drew up the rules for a convalescent fund, to which a number of southern societies had already subscribed. The recommendation to establish a fund instead of building a convalescent home gave considerable interest to the scheme in the light of the opposite decision arrived at in other sections of the Union. This was not a new idea. The Womens' Co-operative Guild already operated a similar fund, which had helped a very large number of its members at a small operating cost and with little red tape.

Since its very early days, the RACS had a few members living north of the Thames who regularly journeyed to Woolwich by the Great Eastern Ferry to

The Links branch, Plumstead 1955

do their shopping at the store in Powis Street. When, in 1881, proposals were made to form a local society, advances were made to the Society for assistance. Alexander McLeod, John Arnold and Tom Chambers assisted in the setting up of the Silvertown Society which subsequently failed, whereupon its members transferred their trade to the RACS. The opening of the Woolwich Free Ferry in 1889 gave impetus to this small amount of trade, and members in that area pressed for a store of their own to save them the inconvenience of crossing the river to make their purchases. As a result of this agitation, the RACS reached a friendly agreement with the Stratford Society to build a store and two houses in North Woolwich. A store with grocery, butchery, and drapery departments opened in October 1905.

Just three months later, the RACS General Committee responded to similar calls from members in Well Hall, Eltham, when a commemorative tablet of the Society's twelfth store was unveiled. The branch consisting of four departments and a reading room was opened in June 1906.

At the central premises in Powis Street, the bakery was extended; new bacon stoves were built; a cooling plant for the dairy was obtained; a coal department commenced; and an optical agency opened with Dolland & Company, upon which full dividend was given.

North Woolwich branch 1949

Urgent appeals for help were also coming from Peckham and Camberwell, and the Society established a branch at Peckham, no doubt influenced by the fact that the London offices of the Amalgamated Society of Engineers were situated there, with staff and members promising support. This area was one of the busiest in London and a shop situated at the junction of Rye Lane and Peckham High Street was opened in November 1907.

The Walworth Society

The prolonged period of depressed trade continued to exercise the minds of the Committee and, with its policy of expansion by merger, it sought to obtain increased support in a wider area. To offset the effect of members leaving the district to seek employment elsewhere and the diminished earnings of those who stayed behind, an approach was made to the Walworth and District Society, with a view to extending operations into its district. This small society was established in 1907, and its 350 members, aware of its lack of capital to expand and develop, agreed to join the RACS the following year, with the result that a shop was opened in the Walworth Road.

Open Air School

Away from the trading scene, considerable interest was aroused in the local and national press by the 'public spirit of the Woolwich Arsenal Society', when it offered its 26 acres of Bostall Wood, in Plumstead, to the London County Council (LCC), to pioneer the experiment of establishing the first open-air school in England, modelled along the lines of 'forest schools' operated in Germany.

The LCC accepted the Society's offer of its woodland, recreation ground and shelter for the school, which was open for three months, from July to September for 120 delicate children. The scholars, suffering from acute anaemia and tuberculosis, were drawn from elementary schools in Woolwich, Plumstead, Greenwich and Deptford, following selection by medical staff. The school ran from 9.00 am to 7.00 pm each day and between 9.00 am and 1.00 pm on Saturday. The LCC had no funds to provide food and clothing for the very poor, and parents were asked to provide contributions according to their means. But this was not sufficient. An appeal was launched for donations towards the costs, approaching £400, which had to be met from sources other than school funds. Little response was obtained, although the target was eventually reached.

The school opened in July 1907 and closed in the following October. The experiment, watched by educationalists and doctors throughout the country, was proved to be a distinct success, with the children showing a marked improvement in their physical condition.

In the following year, the LCC granted the sum of £2,000 in respect of similar experiments at Forest Hill, Shooter's Hill, Plumstead and Kentish Town.

Open Air School, Bostall Woods 1907

Recession and Opposition

The year 1908 was eventful for the RACS in a number of ways. The country and district were still in the grip of recession, and the fortunes of the Society were not in the ascendancy. Sales and dividend rates were on the downturn.

There appeared on the scene a group of 50 or 60 members who decided to form the Royal Arsenal Co-operative Vigilant Committee. They contended that socialism had been allowed to enter the workings of the Society, and it was their intention to secure what they could towards the Society being run on a non-political basis. To achieve this objective, the Vigilant Committee decided to sponsor four candidates in the forthcoming election of the Society's General Committee, and this sponsorship was assisted by circulars issued by the Borough of Woolwich Conservative and Unionist Association.

This decision coincided with a change to RACS rules, which provided for the election of the General and Education Committees to be conducted through polling stations, rather than the members' half yearly meetings. At this first public poll, which was conducted along the lines of a municipal election, there were 14 polling stations which were open from 2.00 pm to 9.00 pm, with each station being manned by a scrutineer and polling clerk. Voting papers were issued on production of a receipt, which was stamped to prevent duplication of voting, and ballot boxes were sealed at the close of the poll and sent to Woolwich. There were 13 candidates for four vacancies on the General Committee. Nearly 3,000 voting papers were issued, which was nearly twice the number issued under the previous arrangements. At that time, the RACS had 26,000 members.

In the event, the four Vigilant Committee candidates were unsuccessful, but the Committee objected to the result, alleging that the Society's employees had distributed papers containing the names of other candidates, which was contrary to the Society's no canvassing rules. In view of this and the circulars of support for the Vigilant Committee candidates issued by the local Conservative Association, the Returning Officer decided that their activities were outside the terms of the Society's rules, and the result should stand.

This episode was followed by a series of rumours, from unknown sources, which were circulated in the district, alleging that the Society's Secretary had absconded with varying sums between £12,000 and £17,000. This was strenuously denied and a reward offered for information leading to the conviction of those concerned with spreading the rumours. All to no avail. Local newspapers were full of the incident, so much so that a number of them decided to suspend correspondence on politics in the Co-operative Society 'until the foolish rumours had been forgotten.'

Differential Dividend

In April 1909, a Special General Meeting was called which approved a recommendation that two or more rates of dividend be paid, one being called the 'general' rate, the other the 'special dividend' which would apply to one department, the bakery. Consideration of the proposal was forced on the General Committee by members making bakery purchases because they wished to receive a greater share in the profits of the bakery department. Members contended that the Society made two profits in its bread business, one in production and another in distribution, and they wished to receive the productive profit, rather than this being added to the general dividend pool for distribution to all members. At that time the general dividend rate was 1s 2d (6p) in the pound and the bakery dividend two shillings (10p) in the pound.

The Imperial Co-operative Society

The same month saw the merging of the Vigilant Committee into a new co-operative society, the Imperial Co-operative Society, with private traders in Woolwich promising their support to the new society. In June, the Society announced in the press that it would be run on similar lines to the Civil Service Supply Association, and that trade union rates would be paid to employees, but members would have no bonuses or any voice in the management of the society. Profits were divided as interest on capital, which was to be limited, and dividend was paid to purchasing members with half dividend to non-members. Business commenced in September 1909, when the Society had 300 members. A shop was opened 'as near to the Arsenal gates as possible', but this was later transferred to 59 New Road, Woolwich. One month later a new rule was adopted which decreed that there would be no politics in the business, no politics discussed at meetings, and no funds would be used for political purposes. A further branch shop was opened at Conway Road, Plumstead, in July 1910, and the Society's six month results revealed sales of £3,853, dividend of 1s 5d (7p) in the pound, and over 700 members. In its report, the committee complained that the Society 'was not getting the support it ought to.'

This new Society had the effect of consolidating RACS membership and, in spite of the continuing depression, sales began to edge slowly upwards. The Imperial Co-operative Society had little impact on the town and was wound up in 1921.

Expanding Influence

The remaining years to the commencement of the First World War saw the RACS moving forward rapidly. In addition to completing the remaining stages of the Powis Street headquarters, branches were opened at New Cross, Catford, Abbey Wood and Peckham; and the passing of the Shop Hours Act, which generally reduced the lateness of shop hours, enabled two hours to be cut from the 50 hour working week.

The South London and Sutton Societies

The policy of expansion through mergers continued. The South London and General Co-operative Society went into liquidation in 1913, and the RACS purchased the whole of its assets, including the lease of its premises, and re-opened its shop in Lambeth at the end of the year.

Raynes Park branch

The following year, the Society was approached by the Sutton (Surrey) District Co-operative Society, to take over its interests at Raynes Park, Wimbledon and Tooting. The RACS sought the opinions of the West London and Penge Societies, which were more closely connected with Sutton, before proceeding. Neither society had any objections and, with the added blessing of the Co-operative Union, the RACS took over the Sutton (Surrey) Society with its 925 members.

The merger created an anomaly with regard to the recording of dividend entitlement. The Sutton (Surrey) Society used the Climax system, which required members to remember and quote their membership number, whilst the RACS used the metal check system. The RACS decided to allow members at the three branches previously mentioned to continue to use the Climax system, 'To ascertain how far it could be used with advantage in other sections of the Society's operations.' At this stage it should be noted that metal checks were issued for deliveries made by roundsmen in this area.

The arrangement was extended in 1922 to include three further branches in the south west area at Earlsfield, New Malden and Colliers Wood; but in 1927 the experiment was discontinued and all branches of the Society issued metal checks. A more detailed account of how these checks were used is contained in Appendix 6.

The RACS area of operations expanded rapidly and it was inevitable that questions of boundaries with neighbouring societies kept cropping up. After friendly discusssions, boundary agreements were made with Penge and Beckenham, the West London and the Dartford Societies. Early in 1913, this improved co-operation enabled societies in Greater London to act in concert when reaching an agreement with the Bakers' Union to avert a bakers strike throughout the whole of the London area. This incident led to

Earlsfield branch

the formation of a London Joint Committee, to which each affiliated society sent three delegates to monthly meetings, where matters affecting London co-operators were discussed, and united action taken if at all possible.

The policy of linking up with societies already in existence became a fashionable subject for conferences. Official reports contained schemes of amalgamation, but, in the main, the problem to be solved was how to secure success by the linking up of one weak society with another weak society. As a result, few schemes came to fruition. In the course of the years, Chislehurst, Crays Industrial and Sevenoaks had joined Bromley; Caterham, Sutton and Epsom had joined Croydon; and Brixton and Norwood had merged with Penge. But the only amalgamation was of Bromley with Crays Industrial in 1908 when the new society became the Bromley and Crays Society, with Cray members entitled to representation on the management committee.

CHAPTER 4
EDUCATIONAL ACTIVITY: 1878 to 1914

ROYAL ARSENAL CO-OPERATIVE SOCIETY: 1878 - 1914

The Co-operative Movement has never been solely concerned with economic objectives. From the Rochdale Pioneers through to the Christian Socialists, education has been seen as an important task for co-operators.

Early Days
The founders of the RACS considered that their most urgent educational need was for personal enlightenment regarding the Co-operative Movement. Many of them were skilled engineers and members of the Amalgamated Society of Engineers, which had close connections with the Christian Socialists, for whom education was a prominent objective. It was logical therefore that these RACS pioneers should follow the example of the Rochdale Society and set aside 2½ percent of the trading surplus (profit) for the education of members.

The first RACS Education Committee of 11 members was elected in 1878, following a recommendation of a rules revision committee set up three years earlier. The Committee was subordinate to the General Committee, and the Society's rules provided that, '(The Education Committee) shall not be allowed to vote away any portion (of the education grant) to be spent or disposed of by any other party'. The first grant amounted to £20 10s 6d (£20.52½p).

The Education Committee's first activity was a social evening for the benefit of the South Wales Miners' Distress Fund held at the Nelson Street Lecture Hall in Woolwich on 15th May 1878, when the aims of the new Committee were outlined by prominent members of the General and Education Committees. They were supported by Edward Owen Greening, a regular speaker at the Society's gatherings and a resident of South East London, who spoke of the moral advantages of co-operation. At that time, the Society had 883 members, capital of £3,323 and an annual trade of £18,976. The dividend was 1s 6d (7½p) in the pound.

CO-OPERATIVE BANNERS

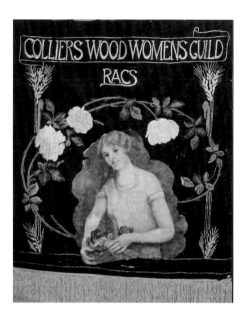

RACS Colliers Wood Branch, CWG

RACS Kingston-on-Thames Branch, CWG

National Music Festival

SSCS Bellingham Branch, CWG

Pioneering Work

In those days, public libraries were few and far between and a number of societies had established libraries and reading rooms for members. In 1879, the RACS provided a reading room in Powis Street, where daily and weekly newspapers and magazines were available along with a number of high-class reviews. A library of 700 books was also opened at the Central Premises at Woolwich in the same year. Subsequently, other reading rooms were opened and these were followed by lending libraries at Charlton, Erith, Belvedere, Abbey Wood, Well Hall, and Peckham, although these were gradually closed in later years, as local authorities with their greater resources took over this role.

In spite of keeping up links with the education work of the Co-operative Union and other local Christian Socialist organisations, the work of the Education Committee in the 1880s tended to emphasise propaganda and membership recruitment rather than co-operative education. The General Committee tried to pressurise them into work of a propaganda nature, but limited resources prohibited them from taking up social issues. Nevertheless, regular educational visits were undertaken, a choral society was formed in Woolwich in 1882 and, four years later, lectures on geography were arranged. These were followed in 1887 by a study circle on the History and Principles of Co-operation using the text book *Working Men Co-operators* by Ben Jones and Arthur Acland.

The activities of women, particularly the Womens' Guild, became more influential, which resulted in Mary Lawrenson and Elizabeth Sheldon being the first women elected to the Education Committee in 1884.

In 1890, the first junior choir was formed, which led later to the Junior Circle. A year later, an oxy-hydrogen lantern was purchased so that lectures could be illustrated, thus commencing a policy of providing visual aids, and culminated in the Education Department possessing lanterns, visual projectors, epidiascopes, episcopes, kodascopes, a De Vry 16mm sound projector and a mobile unit to convey the equipment to lectures.

Wider Interests

From the early 1890s, the Society's educational work took on new dimensions, developing links with local political and trade union movements, and a growing interest in education with a political relevance. This was pioneered by Charles H Grinling, a Christian Socialist, who came to Woolwich in 1889 after several years of social work at Toynbee Hall and Nottingham. He became secretary of the local Charity Organisation Society and helped establish the Woolwich Branch of the University Extension Association. These activities brought him into contact with the RACS and he served on the Education Committee from 1895 to 1898, during which time the Society ran its education work in co-operation with the UEA, the Woolwich Polytechnic and the London School Board.

Comradeship

To maintain contact with members, the Education Committee launched its local co-operative magazine with the masthead of *Comradeship*, under the editorship of Grinling. The publication appeared quarterly from 1897, changing to monthly from 1901, the same year that the Woolwich Baptist Tabernacle was purchased and renamed the Co-operative Institute. The magazine was essentially social in character, aiming to promote co-operative ideals and wide ranging discussion on local and national education, social and industrial issues. Over the years, its content and effectiveness varied according to its editors, amongst whom were Henry J May, who was later to become General Secretary of the International Co-operative Alliance (ICA), Dr Gilbert Slater, a lecturer at the Woolwich Polytechnic and later Principal of Ruskin College, Oxford, and Joseph Reeves, the Society's Education Secretary and later Secretary-Manager of the Workers' Film Association. From a provocative, thought provoking and sometimes contentious magazine, it developed, during the later years into a communications journal, amalgamating in 1922

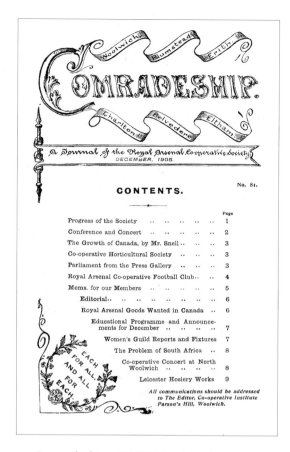

Comradeship - RACS Members Magazine

with *Wheatsheaf*, the organ of the CWS, which provided topics with a broader base whilst retaining the individuality of *Comradeship*. By 1910, the circulation of the magazine had reached 7,000 due to demand from the greatly increased membership.

Of the three editors named above, the first, Henry J May, is best remembered for his sterling work for the ICA through the difficult First World

H. J. May, 1867-1939

War period and the traumatic years building up to the Second World War. Before starting work in the Woolwich Arsenal as an engineer, he was employed for a short period around 1900 in Brewery Road, Plumstead, branch. There, he came under the influence of Alexander McLeod, and his 'enthusiasm for ideals, zeal for service, and honesty of purpose' was nurtured. May served on the Society's General Committee and later entered full-time service with the Movement as Secretary of the Southern Section of the Co-operative Union and later Secretary of the Parliamentary Committee. He joined the ICA as General Secretary in 1913.

Widening Horizons

In 1900, the Co-operative Womens' Guild held its Congress in Woolwich. The slump following the Boer War brought about a reduction in the Education grant, and it did not reach the £1,000 mark until 1911.

The RACS Horticultural Society was formed following successful flower shows in 1903 and 1904. By 1910, five Junior Guilds had been formed and, in the same year, 100 propaganda meetings had been arranged.

At that time, the Education grant was spent on attracting people to join the Society and extolling the benefits that membership offered to them. It was not until the end of the First World War that adult education was undertaken.

SOUTH SUBURBAN PRECURSORS: 1860-1914

Although the South Suburban Co-operative Society was not formed until 1918, its constituent societies undertook their early educational work along similar lines to their neighbours in Woolwich. They spread the gospel of

South Suburban Letterhead

co-operation by providing speakers at public meetings, arranged lectures and discussions on social issues, and made books available for their members before municipal libraries became established.

Each Society appointed or elected a separate committee to undertake these tasks, although the small amounts of money allocated for the work hardly warranted their existence. The Croydon Education Committee was elected in 1896, but grants to education from 1888 to 1902 did not reach £50.

Reigate Society marked the opening of its first store with a celebration meeting at the Town Hall in 1863, and this type of meeting was popular with most societies throughout the area, continuing in some places until 1920. Brixton, Norwood and Penge Societies held regular concert meetings and musical evenings – some before 1880 – and Lloyd Jones, George Jacob Holyoake, E O Greening, Ben Jones, Judge Hughes, Hodgson Pratt and J T W Mitchell were among those who visited the societies to spread the co-operative message and recruit new members. As early as 1883, Penge made a room at the shop available for social and recreational activities and, when the new shop was built at Green Lane in 1901, provision was made for a hall. Halls and meeting rooms were also provided at Norwood (1874), Bromley (1887), Epsom (1896) and Caterham Valley (1899).

Publications and Libraries

The Movement's journals were also well promoted. *The Co-operator* published by Henry Pitman in the 1880s had a fair circulation, and *Co-operative News*, first published in 1871, was also well supported – the Crays Industrial Society distributing free copies at Christmas and having a regular order of six dozen copies each week in 1888. The Brixton, Bromley and Crays Societies also subscribed to *The Metropolitan Co-operator* (1876-1897), a journal of eight pages edited by William Openshaw, one time Chairman of Brixton Industrial Education Committee.

An outstanding feature of the 1880s was the provision of lending libraries of varying sizes at Penge, Crays, Bromley, Caterham, and Reigate at a time when there were no municipal libraries. Outings to the seaside also became popular events with a number of societies, with Margate and Sheerness as popular venues.

Expanding Influences

The period from 1900 was one of trade expansion and co-ordination, and education activities reflected the changes. There was a greater sense of urgency in making provision for social education and propaganda and, in spite of a number of societies ceasing to exist, education grants became larger as the surviving societies became more successful. For example, the Penge grant increased from £26 in 1910 to £83 seven years later, whilst the Croydon grant went from £35 in 1910 to £162 in 1916. Although many new activities were undertaken – choirs concerts, brass bands, debating societies, dances, flower shows, foreign visits, classes in French, esperanto, and first aid as well as industrial history, co-operation and book-keeping – no great lasting success was achieved, except in the field of music.

The Co-operative Womens' Guild (CWG) was formed in 1883 and, one year later, Mrs Ben Jones formed a West Norwood branch, one of the first six branches to be established nationally. Ten further branches were formed throughout the area, but only Bromley, Croydon, Reigate and Sutton existed until 1920. In many cases, Guild branches were formed by management committees and, in some cases, the Guild operated the Society's drapery business. In the 1900s, the CWG took up serious consideration of social, political and economic problems. The Norwood branch had three Guild members on its Management Committee in 1895, and, in 1902, Croydon had two members on its Board and one on the Education Committee.

CHAPTER 5
THE CHALLENGE OF
WORLD WAR 1

As in previous times, prosperity returned to the Woolwich area with the outbreak of war in August 1914. Many members of the RACS were employed in the Woolwich Arsenal, and they were advised by the Society through its members' magazine, 'To put a bit by for a rainy day. The boom will not last for ever.'

Supply Difficulties

The Society and its members suffered inconvenience by the requisition of its horses and motor vehicles for military service, and the early months of the war saw a rush for goods by those who foresaw shortages in the pipeline. However, the resolute stand taken by societies not only in London but throughout the country, by allowing their own members to have their normal weekly supplies, along with a policy of not raising prices unless absolutely unavoidable, kept control over a difficult situation. Societies were helped in their task by the operations of the CWS which continued to supply goods at lower prices than the Government list. When flour prices were increased after existing stocks became exhausted, they announced their intention to bear the extra cost as a war risk. This experience made societies resolve to do all in their power to keep prices down, even if dividends were to suffer. They also learned that they would have to try and control the sources of supply of 'the necessities of life', to avoid the exploitation of the middleman. Thus, federation in districts, and ultimately nationally, was the objective.

The year 1915 saw the RACS continuing the policy of low prices, with the resumption of grocery deliveries to outlying districts. Supplies of basic commodities were still difficult, especially milk and coal which were delayed due to problems on the railway.

At the beginning of the year, 1,000 houses had been built on the Bostall Estate but the work had to cease due to the heavy increase in the price of material. Three houses in McLeod Road on the estate were furnished and occupied by various families of Belgian refugees. The expense of furnishing was offset by contributions from members and employees raised at various functions organised by the Education Committee. The Woolwich Borough Council, and gas and water utilities were also generous in their support. The Co-operative Union also made a grant from its national fund, which was allocated between the refugees housed in Woolwich and those similarly housed in Wimbledon.

An institution was provided for soldiers near the Bostall Estate, and was opened in Federation Hall. It was furnished with games and writing materials, and refreshments were provided from the Abbey Wood Co-operative Women's Guild. The Education Committee was also arranging entertainment for wounded soldiers in the War Memorial and Brook Hospitals.

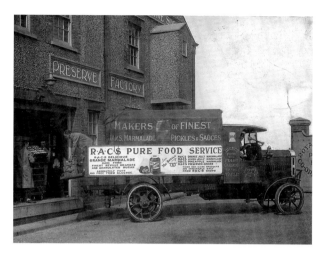

RACS Preserve Factory

1915 also witnessed the opening of new shops at Bexleyheath and Crofton Park as well as the laying of the foundations of the jam factory at Blithdale Road on the Bostall Estate and a new productive bakery at Brixton.

The following year saw a continuation of the difficulties in obtaining supplies. Sugar seemed to be causing particular aggravation. The Government's Sugar Commission refused to increase the RACS sugar allocation in spite of the increasing numbers of members, who were mainly immigrant munition workers, with the result that the Society, in the interests of equity and following agitation by its members, decided to ration its sugar. The Jubilee History of the RACS records the system that was introduced some nine months before a Government scheme. Members who had returned checks to the value of £2 to £10 in the previous half year were entitled to receive 1lb of sugar each week, and members who had returned checks amounting to over £10 received 2lbs each per week. This move caused a question to be raised with the Chancellor of the Exchequer, in the House of Commons, asking him to direct the Society to stop the practice. He refused to do so.

Taxation

For many years, powerful trading interests had advocated the assessment of co-operative societies to income tax and, during 1916, increased efforts were made to bring this about. This agitation created confusion in the minds of members and, to clarify the position, reference was made in *Comradeship* – the Society's magazine – to a tax form issued by the Board of Inland Revenue which required members to declare 'income from any dividends and interest you receive, including share interest or deposit interest from co-operative societies.' *Comradeship* pointed out this was the first occasion that savings of the working classes had appeared on any return of this type, and a protest was made to the Board of Inland Revenue on behalf of the Co-operative Movement. This resulted in the editor of *Comradeship* publishing an extract from a letter from the Inland Revenue dated 17th July 1915: 'Dividends on purchases made by members of co-operative societies are not assessable to income tax, and it is

45

Northumberland Heath branch 1940

not intended that they should be included in the Statement of Income.'

The year 1916 was one of continued trading progress, in spite of a reduction in shop opening hours in Woolwich; the opening of the Preserve Factory and a branch shop at Northumberland Heath, and the appointment of William Baker Neville as Secretary of the Society, succeeding T George Arnold who was elected to the full-time Board of the CWS.

The Chairman of the General Committee paid the following tribute to Arnold on his resignation, as reported in *Comradeship* in September 1916:

Mr T George Arnold J P was born at Greenwich on March 11th, 1866, being now in his fifty-first year. In the very early days of the Royal Arsenal Co-operative Society his father (Mr John Arnold) became an active member of the Society, and served on the General and Education Committee. Mr Arnold had thus the advantage of commencing his career in a co-operative atmosphere. His early education was received at the New Road Presbyterian School, Woolwich at that time under the headmastership of the late Mr John Russell, a gentleman of varied and powerful attainments. At the age of 14 (in February 1880) Mr Arnold was, after a competitive examination, appointed as the first office boy under the guidance of the late Mr McLeod. Thenceforward Mr Arnold's progress and that of the Society proceeded in unison until in March 1889, when, in order to cope with the greatly increased business, Mr Arnold was, on the recommendation of the late Mr McLeod, appointed to the position of assistant secretary to the society. In the year following (1890), his first literary effort appeared, when in collaboration with Mr McLeod he wrote the History of the Royal Arsenal Society for the coming-of-age celebrations, which was subsequently rewritten for the Handbook of the Co-operative Congress held at Woolwich in 1896. On the death of Mr McLeod in 1902, Mr Arnold was

T. G. Arnold,
RACS Secretary

appointed Secretary of the Society, from which position he has now resigned to take up duties as a director if the Co-operative Wholesale Society Limited.

Besides his adminstrative duties, under which the Society grew considerably, he was active in the wider Co-operative movement and served on the Woolwich Council and the LCC.

Rationing

As a result of anomalies in its earlier system of rationing sugar, in January 1917, the Society adopted the procedure of issuing Sugar Cards to its 50,000 members. The Daily News of 2nd February reported that, '(The Society's) sole

Eltham Park hutment shop (RACS) 1917

aim is to distribute in an equitable manner the supplies we receive. We shall not in future deliver sugar to order. All quantities must be applied for personally and taken away.' Sugar was distributed on the basis of purchases. Members who spent from £2 to £4 during the past six months received cards entitling them to half a pound of sugar weekly. Those who spent £5 to £13 got 1lb a week and for £14 and more the quantity allowed was 2lb. There was a limited supply for non-members. This expensive operation to ensure equity of supply was later recognised by the Government, and was the forerunner of a food registration system, completed by the Society, which rationed an additional nine basic commodities. This drastic action became necessary due to the considerable influx of war workers into the district which, coupled with shortages of supply, created food shortages. A deputation to Lord Rhondda, the Food Controller, was successful in obtaining larger supplies for the district. The Coalition Government was slow in providing a suitable food rationing scheme, and there is no doubt that the experience gained by the Society was of help to the Ministry of Food when it introduced official rationing in 1918.

Whilst all this was going on, the Society had to contend with a threatened major strike of its employees, concerning the payment of war bonus, and this was ultimately settled at arbitration. But it still found time to convert three bungalows to two branch shops for the convenience of government workers on hutment estates at Welling and Well Hall.

The end of the war in 1918 also saw the Jubilee of the Society, which was marked by a special commemorative gathering of representatives of local societies. At that time, the RACS was in contact with approximately 10 per cent of the population in an area which extended for 25 miles from Erith in Kent to Raynes Park in Surrey. Its capital was approaching £850,000 and its annual trade was over £2 million.

Of course the South Suburban Society had not yet been formed, but the new economic and social problems brought about by the war created an impetus to the birth of stronger co-operative organisations. The strongest urge for the new society came from the Bromley Society with lesser degrees of enthusiasm from Croydon and Penge. After the defeat of the federal bakery proposal, Penge thought that fusion was a dead issue, but Bromley persisted. The three societies came together again in 1915, and members' meetings endorsed the general agreement to go ahead, by the formation of a sub-committee to formulate proposals. Negotiations on the scheme of arrangement, the first committee and officials took three years to complete, and the South Suburban Society came into existence on 31st July 1918.

CHAPTER 6
THE POLITICAL RESPONSE:
THE FORMATION OF THE
CO-OPERATIVE PARTY

Shortage of supplies of essential food and meat were the order of the day in 1918. The Government introduced a scheme of rationing at the beginning of the year, and the RACS introduced its own meat rationing scheme to ensure supplies to its members.

National Agitation
The departure from the Rochdale principle of political neutrality became necessary in view of the treatment meted out to societies on such matters as income tax and unfair representation on food control committees. The national mood of the majority of co-operators for political representation can be judged from an article in the July 1917 edition of *Comradeship* which stated: 'The way in which the people have been fleeced during the past three years, the gross iniquities which have been placed on co-operators' shoulders, the attempts, secret and open, to injure our cause, have convinced the majority that in self defence we must be represented there (Parliament) and the Congress voiced its decision for this.' Thus, at the Swansea Co-operative Congress, the Co-operative Party was born.

Local Differences of View in the RACS
However, the RACS General Committee took the view that the Society's position was greatly different from that of the majority of societies, by reason of the area covered – from Erith to Wimbledon – and the many constituencies – numbering 22 – touched in the several counties in which it operated. This was a complex problem and any local scheme of work would have to be supported by substantial grants from the Society's members. Briefly, the scheme involved the setting up of local Constituency Organisational Committees (COC) and a central advisory committee partly nominated and partly elected from the COCs and the Society's standing committees to deal with the work of securing direct representation of co-operators. The constitution, powers and duties of these bodies were outlined as a basis for general discussion. A series of conferences were held to consider the merits of both sets of proposals, but there was the general feeling that the Society should go it alone with its own direct representatives,

although there were rumblings from influential members that there should be a tie up with the Labour Party. In view of this, the Society pulled back from its scheme and, at its half-yearly meeting held in March 1918, members approved, by a postal vote, a grant £120 to go to the Co-operative Union's Central Fund for Political Representation. (This followed a grant of £500 at the previous meeting to the *Woolwich Pioneer*, a local Labour newspaper.)

At the following quarterly meeting, the setting up of a local political fund was again proposed but, again, it was defeated.

The strengthening of Labour Party activity, not only in the Woolwich area but in the other districts of South London recently incorporated in the Society's trading area, began to bring more radical and vocal political views from the Education committee – so much so that the General Committee 'blue pencilled' an article in *Comradeship* written by Joseph Reeves a young journalist and a member of the Committee on the question of the Labour Party affiliation. In retaliation, the Education Committee resolved to discontinue the publication of *Comradeship*, but later rescinded this decision on the appointment of Reeves as Education Secretary. (Arthur Hainsworth had just resigned the post to take up the appointment as Metropolitan District Organiser for the Co-operative Union). Reeves appointment did not please the General Committee which was adopting a cautious approach to political work.

Joe Reeves RACS Education Secretary
(seated on desk)

The work of the Education Committee in the two years ending in 1921 concentrated on political propaganda, with the editorials of Reeves in *Comradeship* emphasising the policy. A members' conference in 1919 revived the subject of co-operative political representation and, at the half yearly meeting in March 1920, a members' proposition to revise the Society's rules to allow political representation was approved by 1,500 votes in favour and 47 against. A special committee was set up to revise the Society's rules, and the resultant majority report, which recommended a single Parliamentary candidate, and minority report, which proposed allocating the political fund over the whole of the Society's area, were considered at members' meetings in May 1921. Whilst both reports supported direct affiliation to the Labour Party, members decided to adopt the proposals of the minority report.

Thus, the Political Purposes Committee was born, to promote the Society's political aims and interests and to administer a fund which was to be established by an allocation from the Society's surplus equal to 3d per member, excluding any member who objected to the payment.

South Suburban Supports Congress Decision

However, the constituent societies making up the South Suburban Society were adopting a different tack. All three had supported the Swansea Congress decision to secure direct representation of co-operators in Parliament, and they had given funds to the National Co-operative Representation Committee (later to be known as the Co-operative Party) and formed local groups.

Whilst Bromley and Penge had always been active in seeking representation on local authorities, there was a greater conflict of opinion in Croydon between the Society and the Labour Party, although committee members had contested local government elections as Labour candidates.

After the amalgamation, the Rules Committee was asked to consider the Society's policy on Parliamentary and local representation. It was decided that it was impractical to take action on Parliamentary representation – the area covered twelve constituencies, all of which were usually controlled by the Conservatives. As far as local representation was concerned, it was decided not to set up separate machinery to contest elections but to form local Co-operative Party Councils to keep an eye on co-operative interests.

A Central Co-operative Party Council was also formed, consisting of members of the Management and Education Committees, the Guilds, the local councils and a number of elected members. Local councils were to be formed as approved by the Central Council which was given a grant of £100 to carry out its work. The establishment of local committees turned out to be difficult – only six were formed by 1920 – and the first report of the Central Committee referred mainly to activity involving members who were sponsored by local Labour Parties.

The enthusiasm of local committees waxed and waned and, on occasions, there were no contests for representation on the Central Council. Members of the Society who contested local elections on behalf of the Labour Party were given assistance by publicity to members of the Society in the wards concerned. Independent co-operative candidates were few.

CHAPTER 7
THE EXPANSION OF THE RACS:
1919 to 1939

Post-war Problems

The 20 year period between the two World Wars saw the success of the RACS become less dependent upon the fortunes of the Woolwich Arsenal. The Society's expansion policy provided it with a trading area from Slade Green in Kent to Chessington in Surrey, and it was this development that enabled it to cope more adequately with the usual post-war problems of

RACS Chessington branch

unemployment, distress and rising prices. There is no doubt that the Society's policy during the early 1920s of keeping bread and milk prices down to the lowest possible level proved to be of great value to South Londoners.

This is borne out by the following extract from the 1925 Interim Report of the Royal Commission on Food Prices which said:

> The attitude of the Co-operative Societies to price-fixing is interesting. Witnesses from these societies have informed us that they are frequently approached by the local master bakers with suggestions that the price of bread should be raised. The witness from the Woolwich Royal Arsenal Co-operative Society stated that during the years 1922 to 1924, the bread prices of his society were on average a half-penny to one penny lower than the official London prices fixed by the London Master Bakers' and Confectioners' Protection Society. It appears to be the case that Co-operative Societies do very often, owing to their refusal to act with the local master bakers, keep down the price of bread to the benefit not only of their own members but also of their rivals' customers.

All four London societies also cut the price of milk, contending that there was no justification for charging winter prices in the late spring.

Constitutional Changes

The Society's expansion had made it the fourth largest distributive society in the UK, and in view of this and its future expansion of operations, a review of its administration was undertaken, with the result that the General Committee recommended to members in March 1919 that it manage the affairs of the Society on a full-time basis. Numerous conferences and meetings were held to discuss the Society's proposals, which were finally approved a year later, but it was not until March 1921 that the full-time General Committee took over the management of the Society. The RACS was the only retail co-operative society to have a full-time General Committee, and this arrangement continued until 1978. Then it reverted to part-time, as part of an agreement to secure a merger with the South Suburban Society, which in the event did not take place.

We cannot pass on without mentioning another tremendous change in the Society's democratic process, namely the introduction of proportional representation with the transferable vote, for the election of the Society's General and Educational Committees and Delegates to Co-operative Congress. Model ballot papers on this new system of voting by numbers were published in *Comradeship* several months before the election in 1921, with the objective of educating everyone in the principles of PR. It is not the intention to describe in detail the ramifications of the system – the lay members' difficulty in understanding its workings is perhaps the main disadvantage – but, apart from this, it served the Society well. (See Appendix 5.) It ensured reasonable continuity in the management, outside districts could secure representation if they wished, and it made it more difficult for electoral groups to obtain a majority on a committee to secure their own ends and purposes. Voting by numbers, which is required by the system, could encourage 'plumping' for a single candidate – but this could be of disadvantage to the candidate as papers could not be transferred because sufficient next choices or preferences were not shown on the paper.

Shornells

To mark the Society's Jubilee in 1918, members of the Society approved the purchase of 11 acres of woodland and a house, known as Shornells, which adjoined the Bostall Woods in Plumstead, south east London. The house was the home of a well-known Woolwich architect and had been used as a convalescent home for wounded officers during the war. The Society used the house for educational purposes as well as a rest home for members and, over the years it proved to be a popular venue for all types of member activity, having a special place in the hearts of numerous members both locally and nationally. Unfortunately, the property was burnt down by vandals in 1988 and, from its ashes, a small hospice has arisen – thus the wheel has turned full circle in caring for the sick.

Shornells, RACS Education Centre

The first year of the next decade opened with the possibility of a further extension of the Society's area. The West London Society, with its headquarters in Fulham and branches on both the south and north banks of the Thames, initiated discussions with the Society on a possible fusion. A joint committee was set up to review the position and after several months of discussions, the West London Society decided that a merger could only proceed if the new society had a different name and that it was guaranteed representation on the new Board for two years. The RACS was not prepared to accept these pre-conditions, with the result that the West London Society withdrew from the discussions, and commenced negotiations with the newly-formed London Co-operative Society. From a report issued to West London Society members, it was clear that it was already talking to the London Society during its discussions with the RACS, whose General Committee took the view that the failure of negotiations was directly attributable to the London Society. In the event, West London merged with the London Society in 1921.

New Ventures

The period to 1930 saw sweeping changes in the Society's operations. The purchase of two charabancs in 1920 began the venture into the travel and coach business. Two years later, death benefits and staff training schemes were introduced, followed in 1923 by an Easy Payments System (an instalment plan to enable members to purchase higher priced furniture, hardware and electrical items).

Basque refugee children arriving in RACS coach at Shornells

In 1925, the RACS purchased a 90 acre Government housing estate at Well Hall, Eltham, for £375,000 and renamed it 'Progress Estate'. It was in 1915, with the influx of workers into the Woolwich Arsenal, that a serious shortage of houses had to be faced. The provision of the houses was a military requirement, and speed in their erection was of paramount importance. The work commenced in February 1915, and finished on December 11th in the same year and, in this short period, nearly 1,300 houses and flats were built at a cost of over £800,000, making provision for a population of 6,500. Separate contractors were appointed for roads and houses, and 36 sub-contractors were employed, all of whom employed over 5,500 men on the work. When the estate opened there was a waiting list of

Sandby Green, Progress Estate

1,700 families applying for accommodation. A hall for the use of residents was built in November 1935. The estate operated as a subsidiary company of the Society until November 1980, when it was sold to a housing association.

For many years, co-operative societies stood out against credit trade, but the startling success achieved by the London and South Suburban Societies with their Mutuality Club trading in the dry goods and coal businesses prompted the RACS to introduce a similar scheme in 1926. Over 200 collectors were appointed and, after one month, more than 15,000 members had joined the club and over £27,000 of vouchers had been issued. The introduction of the scheme had also encouraged 4,000 members to join the Society in the first six weeks of its formation. At roughly the same time, members agreed unanimously to the establishment of an Employees' Superannuation Fund.

A Mutuality Club Agent Calls

In December of the same year, negotiations were concluded with the Admiralty for the sale to the Society for £60,000 of nearly nine acres of freehold land and buildings in what was formerly the Royal Dockyard on the Thames at Woolwich. Initially, the Society took over the whole of the frontage to Albion Road and Trinity Street, Woolwich; and at a later date (August 1927), it acquired a further six acres including waterside frontage. The site has a remarkable history of its own, including a dockyard in which Tudor warships were built, and underground tunnels used during the Napoleonic Wars to move French prisoners from the prison ships on the Thames to work on the mainland.

The RACS purchased this site with the intention of using it for industrial purposes, incorporating dairy, laundry, footwear repairing, tailoring, warehousing and garaging services. At its peak, 1,500 people were employed there. To mark the event, a great co-operative exhibition was held in March 1927 in the Dockyard, now renamed Commonwealth Buildings, under the auspices of the Society and CWS. The exhibition created enormous interest. Over 34,000 new members were recruited during the two weeks. Apart from the many stands containing CWS productions, lectures, sketches, choirs, concerts and processions provided entertainment for the estimated 100,000 who attended the exhibition. Amongst the visitors were His Royal Highness, the Prince of Wales – one of the Society's landlords (the Society had a branch in Kennington Lane, which was part of the Duchy of Cornwall estate) – and the Home Secretary, Sir William Joynson-Hicks.

1928 saw the pharmacy business introduced into the Society's operations – later, for legal reasons, to become a subsidiary company – and, a year later, the funeral furnishing and laundry services were inaugurated.

Away from the trading scene, a referendum of employees was taken in 1927 on proposals to set up machinery which would enable them to make known their point of view on matters in which they were intimately concerned, which had to be decided by management. The result was a large majority in favour of the establishment of a Workers' Advisory Council, which was representative of

Commonwealth Buildings Main Gate, 1927

all sections of employees with the objective of considering matters affecting their welfare and the interests of the Society. The Council was able to pass its views on trade, education of employees and disciplinary matters, and a Joint Advisory Council of the General Committee and members of the WAC met monthly. The JAC also promoted social activity and provided for the employees' welfare, but it was not concerned or involved with trade union negotiations.

Funeral of Mr R. Wale RACS Chairman passing through Bostall Estate 1934

In addition to making the two major purchases of Progress Estate and Commonwealth Buildings, the RACS acquired in 1927 the drapery and furnishing business of Grose Brothers, in the Walworth Road, and the 70-year-old establishment of Strouds Limited, Lewisham (later rebuilt and called Tower House), both in south east London, and this brought its total expenditure to near half a million pounds. All this was in addition to sending £10,000 for the relief of distress in mining areas during the general strike. At that time, the Society's annual trade was £4.3 million, with a membership of 145,000 and paying a dividend of 1s 6d (7½p) in the pound.

Early branches of the Society were built with meeting rooms to enable members to have their own facilities and overcome the difficulty of finding suitable accommodation for their activities. In December 1925, members agreed that part of the Society's profit should be given to a fund to provide for social and propaganda work. The sum of £2,000 was allocated in January 1926, and a Halls Fund Committee consisting of elected and appointed members was set up in 1928 to administer the Fund. At its peak the Committee administered 29 halls and was responsible for their care and maintenance. The Halls Fund Committee was finally wound up in April, 1980.

Tower House Store, Lewisham

The RACS marked its Diamond Jubilee in 1928 with a celebration at the Royal Albert Hall. A special guest was William Rose, the Society's first secretary, who travelled from his home in Trenton, Michigan, USA. Another important guest was J Ramsay MacDonald MP, leader of the Labour Opposition in Parliament.

CO-OPERATIVE HOUSE, RYE LANE, PECKHAM

Exterior 1953

Café 1932

Arcade 1932

Inner Entrance to Hall 1932

China & Glass department 1932

Large Hall 1955

Expansion in Depression

The general depression of 1929, with widespread unemployment and falling prices continued in 1930 but, despite this, the Society continued to show increases in trade and maintain its policy of expansion. In the ten years to the end of 1929, the RACS had opened a total of 63 new branch shops, specialist food and non-food units.

The grim unemployment situation and continuing poverty showed no general improvement into the 1930s but, in spite of the depressing situation, not one co-operative society had failed and no member had lost any

Surbiton branch 1936

capital. The RACS had managed to increase its trade and carried through its plans to extend co-operative services throughouts its area. Its major department stores in Peckham and Lewisham were reconstructed and services were provided across the area from Blackfen through to New Malden and Morden in Surrey. The Golden West Coach Line was acquired, and its travel business was greatly extended. By 1933, 14 pharmacy shops had been opened, and a laboratory established at Commonwealth Buildings, whilst branches at Surbiton and Tolworth were transferred from the Woking Co-operative Society. Within two years, four further branches had been established in these areas.

The Movement's opponents were still jealous of its dividend distributed to members, and attacks by the press, particularly in London, had the effect of bringing new strength to the Movement. But the 1933 Finance Act made co-operative societies undistributed profit liable to tax, a direct contravention of pledges given by several members of the Government and contrary to all previous taxation policy.

The following year saw a highly successful membership campaign yield over 42,000 new members in six weeks and, in 1935, an Economy Section, along the lines of the bazaars operated by Woolworths and Marks and Spencer, was opened in Eltham. William Baker Neville, the RACS Secretary who introduced this type of trading to the Society, advocated its extension across the Movement, but without success.

Entrance to Eltham
Economy department 1936

59

William B. Neville
RACS Secretary

Another innovation in the same year was the issue of interim dividend vouchers. The difficult economic conditions prompted indications from members that they would welcome the opportunity, when the necessity arose, to receive an interim dividend on the metal checks they had in hand before the usual dividend paying periods came along. It was in October/November 1935, when purchases of winter clothing, footwear and household requirements, e.g. coal, were being made, that it became possible for the first time for members to exchange not less than £5 in brass checks at any one of the five principal district offices at Woolwich, Lewisham, Peckham, Walworth and Tooting. The vouchers acquired in exchange entitled them to obtain goods to the value of the dividend allowed in any dry goods shops. Dividend at that time was 1s 6d (7½p) in the pound, and interim vouchers exchanged also qualified for death benefits. The scheme was remarkably successful and continued until the outbreak of the Second World War.

The Co-operative Movement had made tremendous strides in London in the 1930s, but had not succeeded in opening a store in the prestigious West End shopping area.

William Baker Neville resigned from the Society's service in July 1937 to take up the position of General Manager, London Co-operative Society. Neville had completed nearly 25 years service with the RACS, serving as Secretary of the Society for nearly 21 years. He was born in Nottingham and commenced his co-operative service at the age of 14 with the Langley Mill Society, where he attained the position of office clerk, before leaving to join the RACS.

In paying tribute to Neville's service, F J Comerton, Chairman of the Society, said, amongst other things, 'Nobody in the Society has played anything like the part that Mr Neville has played...in building up the Society to what it is today.' Neville was responsible for the completion of the purchase of Progress Estate; the idea of a central productive establishment in the Woolwich Dockyard renamed Commonwealth Buildings; the acquisition of Grose Brothers, Walworth; Strouds of Lewisham; the planning of Co-op House, Peckham, and the development of the industrial site at Mitcham.

Neville was succeeded as Secretary by F G Burch, who joined the Society from the

Inspecting the barley crop at
Woodlands Farm, Shooters Hill

Reigate office of the Redhill Union Society in 1909. He had been one of the two Assistant Secretaries appointed in 1925, the other being F W Warwick who was later to become General Manager. Burch successfully steered the Society through the difficult years of World War II, and those immediately following, retiring in 1953, after completing 50 years' co-operative service.

The deteriorating situation in Europe and the threat of war caused part of the Woolwich Arsenal to be moved to safer areas. In spite of this depressing scenario, the RACS opened a new laundry at Mitcham, Surrey, and an abattoir at Woodlands Farm, Plumstead, in 1937, followed by an exhibition to mark the Society's 70th birthday the next year. New departmental stores were in the course of construction at Morden and the North side of Powis Street, Woolwich, at the outbreak of World War II in 1939. The Woolwich store opened in stages during 1939 and 1940, but members at Morden did not enjoy the full use of their store until 1948.

Powis Street, Woolwich
(North Side) 1976

Morden department store opening 1938

The Society's sales in 1939 exceeded £10 million for the first time and, during the previous 10 years, it had opened or provided over 70 new shops and services.

The expansion of the RACS away from Woolwich saw the membership grow from 70,000 in 1919 to 382,000 in 1939, the increases being more pronounced during the depressions of 1926-29 and 1932-34.

Educational Activities

The Society's educational resources, linked to its profits, increased nearly five-fold from 1919 to 1937, enabling the Education Committee to expand its activities; provide equipment and premises for classes, drama groups and orchestras; purchase camping gear for young peoples' clubs; and pay tutors and finance scholarships for weekend schools and conferences.

Education work changed in the 1920s, and Joe Reeves, the Society's Education Secretary, asserted that 'the dynamic of education must be altered from individual assertiveness to service on behalf of the community.' Reeves also believed in co-operating with other adult educational bodies in the provision of classes, and took advantage of the 1918 'Fisher' Act to work with the London County Council, the Workers' Educational Association, Ruskin College, Oxford and the Central Labour College.

Cover of Together – RACS Staff Magazine showing the Society's logo

Technical education for employees – also the responsibility of the Education Committee – expanded enormously in the inter-war years, during which time the number of employees increased ten-fold to 10,000. The RACS offered technical education in book-keeping and co-operation, before a scheme was introduced by the Co-operative Union in 1909. After 1918, subjects were taught and scholarships awarded on the basis of Co-operative Union examination results. In the 1930s, all four metropolitan societies got together and organised staff education appointing a joint full-time technical teacher in Salesmanship and Book-keeping. In 1937, the RACS appointed Mr M R Hall as its first full-time Staff Training Organiser. At the outbreak of World War II, the Society was running over 100 classes for staff on technical subjects, and special lecture courses were arranged under the supervision of a Staff Education Council. The following year, a staff magazine *Together* was introduced, and a new education centre at Park Vista, Greenwich, was opened.

The cultural side of the Society's educational work was transformed. There was a tremendous growth of interest in music and drama groups. In 1927, there were 37 musical and dramatic societies operating under its auspices. The Education Department commissioned new works, with a co-operative message, for performance by its own groups.

In 1926, the four London societies set up a London Co-operative Societies' Joint Education Committee (LJEC), and it organised a concert in the Kingsway Hall which was broadcast, and another in the Royal Albert Hall.

The LJEC took over most of the Society's cultural activities, and many of its competition festivals were discontinued in favour of London-wide festivals at Crystal Palace and Caxton Hall.

The RACS Education Department pioneered and encouraged travel after the First World War, and it set up a Co-operative Travel Guild – the first in the country – in 1919, with trips to Belgium and Holland taking place in the following year. Joe Reeves called on the Co-operative Union to set up an organisation for co-operative travel overseas and, in 1922, helped to form the Workers' Travel Association (WTA). From 1927 RACS overseas activity was run jointly by the WTA and LJEC. The RACS was particularly interested in travel to the Soviet Union and it ran tours to the USSR from 1929 until the outbreak of World War II.

After the formation of the National Government in 1931, changes took place in the direction of RACS educational work, brought about by the new political situation facing the labour and co-operative movements, the rise of fascism and the threat of another world war. There was a move away from leisure and handicraft activities to serious social studies, with greater co-operation with the National Council of Labour Colleges and the WEA. The Education Department, in common with the rest of the Movement, strongly supported the peace movement and the Republican cause in the Spanish Civil War. (As part of this, a group of Basque refugee children were housed at Shornells until the end of World War II.) The Department's magazine *Comradeship*, with a circulation of 20,000, promoted discussion on political questions, the problems of war, peace and fascism, which prompted contributions from Stafford Cripps, John Strachey, G D H Cole, Hugh Dalton and many others.

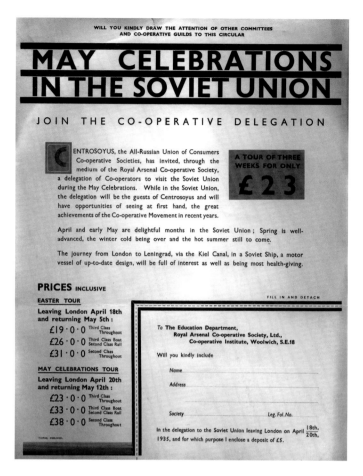

Invitation to visit the Soviet Union 1935

The Members' Council

It was in this period of turmoil and uncertainty that Reeves addressed the question of internal democracy in the Movement, no doubt brought about by the increasing size of the RACS and the reduced member participation to a small percentage of the total membership. In a pamphlet published in 1936 entitled *New Forms of Government in the Co-operative Movement*, Reeves advocated a new system based on a single governing authority – the Members' Council – which would formulate policy to be carried through by sub-committees for management, education and politics, with the aim of bringing back control of the Movement to the members and ending the divisions between the Society's trading, education and political functions. A motion to this effect was considered by a members' meeting in June 1936, but it was rejected. However, following a Rules Revision Committee in 1938, a watered down version, which set up a Members' Council which could only make representations and submissions and was given no power over the Society's other committees, was approved. The First Members' Council was elected on a district basis in April 1939.

Films

The development and potential of films was quickly recognised by Reeves, who did much to introduce this new and developing medium to RACS educational work. In 1931, the Society purchased two films – one from Germany and another from the USSR – which were shown at propaganda meetings as an alternative to concerts. By 1936, more equipment and films had been bought, and an experiment with a sound film was made in 1935. In the 1937-38 season, over 50 film exhibitions were held – with programmes changed weekly – and these included a sound film *Workers Education* made by the Society outlining its educational work. A second film *People with a Purpose* was made in 1939 to illustrate the work of the Society's Education Department in its Jubilee Year. In the wider field, Reeves tried to encourage the Movement to adopt films for educational purposes. In addition to persuading the National Association of Co-operative Education

RACS Film Vehicle

Committees to call national conference to discuss the use of films, he also persuaded the LJEC to grant £1,000 per annum for five years for the purpose of film-making for the Movement. The first film made in 1938 ran for 30 minutes and was entitled *Advance Democracy*. A second film *The Voice of the People* was made in 1940, but the onset of World War II halted the work.

Reeves' interest in films resulted in his 1938 appointment as Secretary of the newly-formed Workers' Film Association, sponsored jointly by the Labour Party and the TUC to encourage the use of films by the Labour Movement.

Thus ended the association between the RACS and one of the foremost co-operative educationalists of the inter-war period. Joseph Reeves founded and encouraged Kibbo Kift Tribes, later to become known as the Woodcraft Folk. The traditional educational work of organising classes greatly expanded during his stewardship, alongside operatic, orchestral and dramatic societies. He was a committed socialist, serving as Labour MP for Greenwich from 1945 to 1959, as well as a profound thinker about co-operation and education and their role in society. He passed away on 8th March 1969 at the age of 81 years.

CHAPTER 8
THE DEVELOPMENT OF THE SOUTH SUBURBAN SOCIETY: 1918 to 1939

Trading

Born in July 1918, the fledgling South Suburban Co-operative Society (SSCS) was not provided with favourable or stable conditions in which to grow. The First World War provoked difficulties in obtaining supplies, restrictions on building, and the loss of experienced staff to the armed forces, whilst the period after the war saw falling prices, rapidly increasing sales and staff returning from the front. Periods of prosperity followed by falling prices and unemployment created a difficult platform to build on. The cost of living index in 1920 was 176 points above that of 1914, but had fallen by 92 points in 1922. The following year saw the beginning of a gradual reduction in the rate of decreases, until increases began in 1923 and these continued until 1930 when another heavy fall in prices was accompanied by general trade depression and unemployment. However, the Society weathered the storm and its foundation led to excellent progress in the 1930s.

At its birth, the Society operated 28 grocery shops with a dozen separate drapery and footwear units, 10 outfitting and four butchery shops along with coal depots and two dairies. The development proposals of the three constituent societies prior to the amalgamation had to be reviewed and new priorities established. Grocery branches were the priority in 1919, and the demand for new shops, through correspondence and by deputation, was provoked by a general increase in

Opening of an early SSCS branch

population and the building of new housing estates at Bellingham, Carshalton, Downham and Morden. This demand was mainly satisfied, but war-time conditions prevented a redress in the over-proportion of grocery outlets to the more profitable dry goods services. Tylney Road, Bromley, was

65

Opening of SSCS Redhill Store in 1935

the first branch to be opened by SSCS in 1919, and this was followed by Wallington in 1920 and Oxted a year later.

Developments and extensions continued until 1929. A single-storey departmental store at Thornton Heath was the first store to provide dry goods departments as well as the traditional grocery and provisions. In 1930, Norwood Road and Sevenoaks provided a similar mix of departments and, in addition, had flats above the shops. More complex multi-floor stores were built at Brixton in 1930 and Croydon two years later, followed by Bromley in 1933, Redhill in 1935, and Penge in 1938.

At the outbreak of the Second World War, there were 75 grocery shops, 15 drapery, 16 outfitting, 16 footwear, 57 butchery, 6 furnishing and hardware, 15 coal depots and 17 dairy depots. 1939 also saw the Society's 21st birthday, but the war prevented any celebration of its achievements and the fact that it had grown to be the fourth largest society in the country.

The established co-operative policy of providing halls and meeting rooms in which members could meet was responsible for the SSCS inheriting seven excellent halls at its foundation, located at Bromley, Catford, Caterham, Epsom, Norwood, Penge and Sutton.

In 1919 and again two years later, members approved at 11 sectional members' meetings the provision of more meeting places, but nothing happened until 1928 when members agreed to the setting up of a Hall Building Fund with a grant of £750 to provide for more halls or rooms. Two years later, members further agreed to establish a committee, made up of elected members and appointed representatives from the management and education committees, along with their officials, which would decide on the location and plans for new halls, leaving the purchase and preparation of plans to the management committee. Following this decision a further seven halls were erected and a further four existing rooms were purchased.

Government and Administration

Quite apart from trading, the new Society's government and adminstration had to be very carefully reviewed. Consideration of its government was put in the hands of a Rules Committee made up of elected members from Bromley, Croydon and Penge along with members of the Management Committee. It produced a report to a special meeting of members in June, 1919, which approved, among other things, four changes: the adoption of the Co-operative Union's model rules; the regulations to be observed in the nomination and election of the President, the Committee and the Society's delegates; standing orders; and the extension of the Death Benefit Scheme to cover members in Croydon and Penge.

Unsuccessful attempts were made, from time to time, to amend the rules. In 1922, a move to extend the Committee's term of office was rejected and, in the following year, the Committee was successful in getting the authority to draft amendments to rule, but not all of these were approved, particularly the proposal to introduce district voting in district elections. Voting by post was rejected in 1929.

It was not until 1932 that the members agreed to elect a Rules Revision Committee. The first report of the Committee in 1933 proposed the setting up of a Members' Council, but this was rejected. A second report three years later outlined the difficulties of presenting a complete revision of rules with members having to submit amendments, and this too was thrown out. 1938 saw another report which proposed another timetable. Special General Meetings were called, but they had to be cancelled due to the number of amendments received. Another meeting was called to approve the rule changes, as submitted, but the proposal was rejected. Nothing happened until 1946, when the Committee announced it would report in 12 months time. Special meetings were requisitioned by members, when proposals were considered to allow unlimited and restricted employee representation on the Management Committee, which were lost, and to allow the adoption of new rules as submitted, which was approved. The new rules included the elimination of districts, a reduction in the number on the Education Committee, its finances, and the establishment of a Co-operative Party Committee. The rules were registered in January 1948 and, in the following May, an attempt to reduce the retiring age of committee members was not accepted, but permission for employees, without limitation, to serve on the Management Committee was given approval by an overwhelming majority. Thus, from the appointment of a Rules Revision Committee in 1932, it took 16 years before a full revision of the rules was completed.

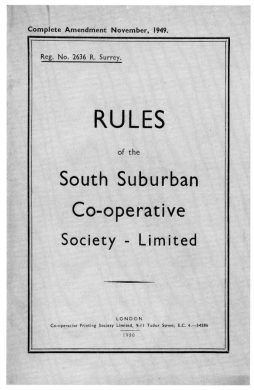

Front Cover of SSCS Rule Book

The administration of the Society compared favourably with the general practice followed throughout the Movement. Up to 1939, Half Yearly Reports and Annual Balance Sheets together with capital and interest statements, were posted to members. After that date, they became available in all district offices and branches. Half yearly members' meetings were held at various locations – by 1938, 18 meetings were being held over four days in one week – although quarterly meetings were usually convened in not more than four venues. The elections of all committees, scrutineers and Congress delegates was conducted by cross vote through polling stations located in shops – there were 79 in 1939 – and polling took place over two days.

Employees

Mention has been made previously of employees who left their societies at Bromley, Croydon and Penge to join the forces in 1914 and the consequent difficulty these societies encountered in providing an efficient service to their members. These employees returned after the war and found their societies had disappeared into the new South Suburban Society, but there was no difficulty in finding them employment in the new set-up.

As early as 1919, a member tried without success to get, 'All employees to become members of their respective trade union recognised by the Trades Union Congress as catering for their respective trades.' The following year, another proposal, 'That all employees over the age of 18 shall be members of a Co-operative Society and members of their respective trade union,' was submitted and this too was defeated. Later in the same year, a two-part proposal was considered by the members. The first requiring all employees over 18 to be members of the Society was rejected; but the second, that membership of a trade union was to be a condition of employment, was carried. This requirement was later to become commonplace, until legislation prevented it in the late 1980s.

Whilst members of the Society were keen on employees being members and trade unionists, they also strongly supported the setting up of a Pension Fund, instructing the Management Committee to do so in 1927. The non-contributory Pension Fund was formed in 1929, and the Joint Pension Committee consisted of elected employee representatives and the management. Benefits from the Fund were conditional upon employees contributing to an Auxiliary Fund to which every employee was eligible to be a member. Pensions payable to retiring employees were made up of amounts due from both funds.

An Employee Benevolent Fund was established in 1939 to provide help during sickness, death or any other circumstance. Employees paid a weekly subscription to the Fund which was administered by elected employees, a member of the Management Committee and an official.

Educational Work 1920-1939

The resolutions setting up the amalgamation of the three societies included one providing for the immediate appointment of a Central Executive Committee, made up of members from each of the three committees, to submit a scheme for the new Society's educational work. An elaborate scheme was presented and rejected, and this was quickly followed by a proposal to elect eight members in each of the three districts, which was accepted in November 1919. An Executive Committee was formed from representatives from each District Committee, the Management Committee and elected members, and this Committee appointed William Stewart as its first full-time secretary. Stewart, who served on the Board of the new Society as a representative from Croydon, commenced his employment in August 1920 and continued in office until 1947.

Left to Right: William Stewart, International Visitor, Jack Halliwell, Publicity Manager, SSCS

At first, it was difficult to get any degree of uniformity of policy between the districts, especially as district decisions had to be ratified by the Executive. In 1926, the districts met as one committee each month, but this did not overcome the frustrations at district level. A special committee was appointed to review the rules and its report of 1930 recommended the Executive Committee be abolished. This was agreed, but the numbers of the combined district committees were increased from 15 to 24. This situation continued until 1947, when the number was reduced to 12 and district representation was abolished.

Considerable time and effort was diverted from educational activities to questions on the constitution of the Committee, but no real progress was possible until 1924/25. When this period was reviewed, one special feature was seen to stand out, namely, the change from propaganda and social activity to formal educational work.

Educational work was financed by a grant from the Society's net profit, and this basis was used from 1920 until 1947, when it was changed to 1¼ per cent of net profit with an additional 3d per member. Funding on this basis fluctuated with the fortunes of the Society, but substantial additional assistance was forthcoming from a number of social committees which arranged very successful dances in the Society's halls.

The Society's roots always had a strong bias for catering for the needs of young people. In 1916, Bromley was one of the few societies to do this. The South Suburban Education Committee continued this work with a policy to find leaders with an aptitude for taking charge of children, coupled with an additional expertise that would interest children. In 1920, nine Junior Guilds with ages ranging from seven to 14 years, later to be named Junior Circles, were meeting regularly and, by 1939, this number had increased to 33 with three choirs.

By 1934, groups of employees and members were undertaking courses of study in various subjects, which included Co-operation and Citizenship and, two years later, a separate booklet was published giving details of classes held and proposals for the next year. In 1938/39, 70 members' and 13 employee classes, which attracted nearly 1,350 students met regularly during the season.

The committee's report to members of September 1938 said:

> The present position enables us to claim that we are now taking a prominent part in adult educational activities in the area covered by the Society. Few organisations, apart of course from Local Authorities, are responsible for such a wide and varied educational programme and we are confident that the persistent efforts of the past years have borne good fruit and have given the Society a definite and recognised place among the educational bodies in the area.

The outbreak of World War II brought a halt to further progress, but a few classes continued to meet during the war in spite of all the problems of being in a direct line for air attacks on London.

Young co-operators camping

The Committee encouraged members of the Circle to take part in local and central displays at International Co-operative Day events, and this was exemplified in 1934 by their participation in a programme at the Crystal Palace, which was in the centre of the Society's area, organised by the London Joint Education Committee for the entertainment of delegates attending the International Co-operative Alliance Congress.

The Society's youth leaders were closely associated with the Co-operative Union when it established the modern co-operative youth movement in 1941.

Senior Guilds became Comrades' Circles in 1921 and were aimed at the 14 to 25 year olds. The British Federation of Co-operative Youth was formed in 1924 and continued until 1941 when it became the British Federation of Young Co-operators with an age range of 18 to 25 years. Between 1920 and 1939, 18 branches were opened, and they provided meeting places and platforms for young men and women interested in economic and political questions.

The South Suburban Society became recognised for its organisation of spectacular events on Co-operators' Day – later to become International Co-operative Day. Childrens' festivals and sports days were popular features, the pioneering event being held at Wallington in 1922. The first visit to Crystal Palace was in 1926, and annual events were held there until 1930, when the venue was changed to Redhill and Sevenoaks. An historical pageant at Crystal Palace in 1931, with over 2,000 performers was watched by over 14,000 who paid for admission. It was repeated in 1932, and a review in *The Review of International Co-operation* stated:

> At the Crystal Palace the South Suburban again produced the historical pageant which was performed by its members last year. And which illustrated the modern social development of England in a vivid and convincing manner, as well as conveying symbolically the co-operative ideal. This pageant, which is the most ambitious yet made in this direction by any British Society, was well worth repeating.

These large-scale events were costly and time-consuming and interfered with the development of formal educational activity. Less ambitious plans were introduced in the following two years, with visits to centres at Downham and Sevenoaks in 1935; but they returned to the 'Palace' in 1936. Junior Circle members visited Littlehampton in 1937, and the Society's adults and juniors provided an episode in the pageant *Towards Tomorrow* staged by the London Society at Wembley Stadium in 1938. Redhill was visited in 1939.

The period between the wars saw additional educational activities in many different forms: choirs, which took part in local concerts and festivals as well as at the Royal Albert Hall; an orchestra, formed in 1927; dramatic groups; members' reunions, of which 49 were arranged between 1928-1939; workers' reunions, from 1928 to 1936; film shows, first mentioned in 1927; gramophone recitals, first established in 1927; flower shows, popular before amalgamation, abandoned during the First World War, but revived in 1924; Arts and Crafts classes; essay competitions; and a students' fellowship with its first branch opening in 1927. In 1934, the group compiled *A Prospectus of the British Co-operative Movement*, which was subsequently published by the Education Committee and was circulated at home and abroad.

In 1920, there were 14 Adult Guild branches, 11 branches of the Co-operative Womens Guild and 11 branches of the Co-operative Men's Guild. By 1939, there were 48 branches of the Women's Guild, nine branches of the Men's Guild and three branches of the National Guild of Co-operators, an organisation established in 1927.

The Society also took an active role in associations and committees concerned with sectional and national educational problems. It joined the other three London societies in the formation in 1926 of the London Joint Educational Committee, for the purpose of establishing uniformity with regard to educational activity, e.g. university extension and tutorial classes, lectures, summer schools, film production and festivals. With a large part of its trading area in Surrey, the Society was a member of the Surrey Joint Education Committee which was formed in 1931. Mr H J Davies was

Chairman for 10 years. The Society was also represented for many years on the Southern Co-operative Education Committees' Association, which was responsible for the development of education in the Southern Section of the Co-operative Union.

The outbreak of the Second World War in September 1939, brought activities to a standstill until, in the words of a circular sent to all groups by the Committee, 'We have experienced the first shocks of actual warfare and have had time to examine the new conditions.'

CHAPTER 9
CONSOLIDATION AND AMALGAMATION - THE CONCEPT OF AN ALL-LONDON SOCIETY

The advisability and ultimate good sense of setting up a single co-operative society for London was clearly established in the minds of progressive, active co-operators in the capital from the early days. There was no doubt that they recognised that London had its special peculiarities and features, which were quite different from anything experienced in the provinces and, on at least one occasion, it was the subject of enquiry by a Joint Committee of the Co-operative Union and the Co-operative Wholesale Society.

Early Discussions

At the Woolwich Congress in 1896, George Hawkins read a paper on, 'Are modifications of the Rochdale system of Co-operation necessary to meet the needs of great centres of population?' when the London problem – societies being started and liquidated or absorbed within a very short time – was specifically and almost exclusively discussed. In the same paper, Hawkins attributed co-operative weakness in London to the movement of the population, the absence of the factory system and the large number of aliens, by which presumably he meant foreign residents.

In November 1913, a conference was convened by the South Metropolitan District Conference Committee in Woolwich, at which T George Arnold, Secretary of the RACS, submitted a paper, 'Co-operation in London: Proposals for Advancement.' Arnold began by referring to the improvement made to trade and transportation in the capital in the previous twenty-five years, and to the continuing failure of co-operatives and family traders in these newer conditions. In the meantime, multiple shops were flourishing 'by the application of more scientific organisation, particularly in matters of salesmanship, advertising, (and) business methods,' developing trade 'on new lines'. He went on:

> Had the co-operative efforts been backed by the same enterprise and business methods as were applied to other efforts, had the signification of the quick turnover and reduced profits been fully realised, with its consequent diminution of dividend, or, more important still, had a high standard of managerial ability and the best trading positions, and not the

limitation of wages or low rents, been considered of first importance, success would most probably have been achieved instead of failures deplored.'

Arnold argued that these matters were more relevant to co-operative failure than those projected by Hawkins 17 years earlier.

He went on to review the trading and financial advantages that multiple retailers enjoyed, and he identified the areas of weakness that affected the competitive position of the 13 distributive societies operating in London. Arnold was of the opinion that this situation could be overcome by the formation of one society for the metropolis – and, if this could not be achieved immediately, a first step could be in the establishment of one society on either bank of the Thames formed by the amalgamation of the seven societies north of the river and the six on the south side. He outlined his suggestions for the financial and managerial arrangements for the new set-up, which included the constitution and powers of a Board of Management elected by the members with a full-time Chairman, and a Board of Managers consisting of senior buyers and departmental and branch managers appointed by the Board and presided over by the Chairman of the Society.

Later, a Mr Coffin argued that the Thames was not a natural barrier to commercial business and advocated one society for London. It was after this that the London Joint Committee of Co-operative Societies was formed to advise the CWS on the requirements and needs of co-operators. Further along the road, a Mr Smith submitted a paper to a Management Committee's conference at Peckham in support of amalgamation, contending the time was ripe for societies to pool their capital, trade and resources. And this was followed by Alfred Barnes, President of Stratford Society, who submitted a paper to another conference of management committees, when he emphasised the necessity and practicability of one society for London.

In May 1920, Barnes again advocated one society for London at another conference held at Peckham, under the auspices of the London District Council of the National Men's Co-operative Guild. This was at a time when the London societies were making rapid progress, when there were over 240,000 members holding capital of over £2.5 million.

In spite of these conferences, where there had been theoretic agreement, no society had submitted the proposal to their members.

The 1928 Co-operative Congress approved a proposal of the Royal Arsenal and South Suburban Societies calling for a large measure of amalgamation 'to meet the growing competition of large capitalist distributive concerns.' This resulted in the Co-operative Union setting up a Committee of Amalgamation – but little happened.

The following year, the Joint Committee of London Co-operative Societies, representing the Management Committees of the Enfield Highway, London, Royal Arsenal and South Suburban Societies, appointed a committee consisting of one member of each of the four Management Committees and one official from each Society under the Chairmanship of Charles Bailey, Chairman of the London Joint Committee.

The Committee's terms of reference were to survey the organisation of the four societies and the present financial position and operations and activities of each of them, in order to enable the advantages and disdvantages of a partial or complete amalgamation to be judged by the members. The Committee was also charged with the duty of making suggestions on

STATISTICAL INFORMATION

POSITION OF THE SOCIETIES IN 1933

	E.H.C.S. Sept., 1933	L.C.S. Sept., 1933	R.A.C.S. July, 1933	S.S.C.S. Sept., 1933	TOTAL.
	£	£	£	£	£
SHARE CAPITAL	579,145	6,467,622	3,227,993	1,770,610	12,045,370
LOAN CAPITAL .... (including penny bank, deposit bonds and clubs)	129,214	896,967	476,147	292,536	1,794,864
Total Capital	708,359	7,364,589	3,704,140	2,063,146	13,840,234
RESERVES— Various Reserve Funds	39,976	207,802	315,850	93,867	657,495
Dividend Equalisation Fund...................	1,397	100,000	122,674	25,000	249,071
Insurance Fund	2,706	81,056	120,756	7,850	212,368
Death Benefits Fund...	4,504	100,000	100,000	6,744	211,248
Total Reserve Funds	48,583	488,858	659,280	133,461	1,330,182
SUPERANNUATION FUND......................	33,318	341,921	234,019	76,183	685,441
LAND, BUILDINGS AND FIXTURES..............	219,439	3,020,177	1,549,300	737,772	5,526,688
PROPERTY NOT USED IN TRADE..............	13,663	52,642	150,635	39,911	256,851
	233,102	3,072,819	1,699,935	777,683	5,783,539
INVESTMENTS	462,874	4,158,931	2,805,551	1,439,711	8,867,067
ANNUAL SALES	875,000	9,821,582	7,009,198	2,815,296	20,521,076
MEMBERSHIP	30,990	486,346	281,010	123,114	921,460
EMPLOYEES	851	11,866	6,773	2,890	22,380
Dividend allocation per £ sales......................	1/3	1/-	1/6	1/6	—
Rate of Interest on Share Capital.........per cent.	$4\frac{1}{6}/3\frac{3}{4}$*	$3\frac{3}{4}$	$4\frac{1}{6}$	$4\frac{1}{6}$	—

* The lower rate of Interest is paid to members whose trade with the society is less than £5 per half-year.

Extract from the Report on the Amalgamation of the Metropolitan Societies, 1934

how closer links or amalgamation between the societies, consistent with the best interest of the Movement in London, could be brought about.

In its final report produced in April 1933, the Committee summarised all the salient details and activities of the four societies, and highlighted the major problems to be solved if the amalgamation was to take place. The most important of these were collective buying and the ability to deal direct in the open market, and, coupled with this, the relationship with the CWS; the payment of bonus on wages to RACS employees and how this would be dealt with in the other societies; differential dividend rates; and management control.

The committee concluded that partial amalgamation to carry out certain services was not favoured and, whilst there were no practical difficulties in the separate fusion of societies north and south of the Thames, they could see no advantage to this partial joining up. They concluded, 'Owing to the complexity of the subject we were not able to arrive at unanimous decisions upon all the suggestions submitted in this Report, and, for the same reason, we do not propose to make any recommendation on the main questions, viz. the desirability of amalgamation.'

Three years later in 1936, William B Neville, General Secretary and Chief Executive of the Royal Arsenal Society, observed, in an article 'Co-operation in London' written for *Tradition*, the house journal of the Co-operative Printing Society, that 'amalgamation as a topical subject has definitely receded.' However in some quarters it was thought that, 'Woolwich and Croydon would have come closer to a final adjustment, if not complete solution, of their demarcation difficulties, and to this end a definite suggestion to fuse the two societies was made by the Woolwich Board; but nothing came of it.' Neville further opined, 'That there does exist a deep-rooted belief that the itch for amalgamation in certain quarters comes not so much from a consideration of economic gain as from political desire.'

Alfred Barnes was a tireless speaker for the fusion of the four London Societies. In February 1929, he addressed a special conference held in the CWS Assembly Hall in Leman Street and outlined the machinery required to 'win the whole of London for Co-operation.' He re-asserted his view that London was one and indivisible. It had a common economic situation, its system of government embraced north and south of the Thames and the needs and desires of Londoners were the same. The only doubt was the speed at which amalgamation could be effected – but it should take place while each society was prosperous.

Role of RACS
The 1930s were a period of intense verbal activity on the amalgamation front. In 1933, Joe Reeves, the RACS Education Secretary, attended numerous one-day conferences throughout the Society's area supporting the amalgamation proposal, but, in doing so, he took the view that the Movement would have

to be transformed completely to meet its capitalist competitors on equal terms. On the matter of democracy and its application to management, he was of the opinion that 'Democracy had almost departed as a method of managing our organisations, and he looked upon the amalgamation of the four societies as a method of re-kindling the democratic flame and giving to this wider trading organisation the means whereby members could once again come into association with those who are elected to manage the organisation.'

Speaking as an ordinary member a few months later, he was critical of the Society's General Committee for 'not giving any official information on the recommendations of a special committee on the amalgamation of the four societies.' He stated that, whilst the London Society was in favour, it was learned that it had been decided not to publish the findings of the enquiry. He asked what were the recommendations; why the time was not right, although amalgamation was agreed; and why members were not given the chance to express their views on the repeated leads given by Co-operative Congress.

At the RACS Annual General Meeting in March 1934, consideration was given to a member's proposition which instructed the General Committee to review negotiations for the amalgamation of the four London societies and, if this could not be achieved, to report back to the members on what partial arrangements could be made. In opposing the motion, the General Committee stated that the time was not opportune for complete amalgamation, but it favoured amalgamation with the South Suburban Society, and it would see how far this was possible. The motion was lost by 694 votes in favour and 1,792 against. The RACS submitted amalgamation proposals to the South Suburban Society, but nothing came of it.

Reeves and John Corina, a member of the General Committee, (later to become Chairman, a member of the CWS Board and President of Congress) continued to support amalgamation. Reeves propounded the advantages of district organisation and greater specialisation, whilst Corina looked at the broader national economic and political future in suggesting 12 or 13 regional societies, each of 600,000 members, with London probably forming one of the regions.

Following the failure of the proposal at the RACS Annual General Meeting, a resolution having the same objective was submitted to each of the other three societies, sponsored by and on behalf of an unofficial body formed for the purpose of promoting amalgamation in London. In response to this, W B Neville, the RACS Secretary, submitted a letter to the editor of *Comradeship* which contained, amongst other matters, comparable statistics of each of the four societies to assist members in their deliberations. Neville asserted that, 'Efficiency, ability to meet competition, and service are more important to London in getting trade, and retaining it, than anything else, and the degree to which efficiency and service could be maintained in an organisation so vast as an amalgamated society would, I feel, depend very largely upon a proper solution of that constitutional problem referred to previously.' (The constitutional problems he outlined were the relationship of committees to the members and the method of selection of the management committee.) He went on, 'It is very doubtful indeed whether that all-important efficiency could be maintained in a vast concern if the management had to be dependent upon the votes of shareholders not understanding the intricacies of modern commerce and the science of business administration, and upon the votes of an active percentage of the membership having a pecuniary interest in the organisation.'

Throughout nearly all of 1937, the columns of *Comradeship* were full of a new tack – federalisation of the metropolitan societies. This was put forward by members as an alternative to amalgamation, although the fundamental principle of the need to come together was never disputed. The federalists took the view that the Movement was failing because member control was prohibited and there was a feeling that nothing of importance could be done regarding policy or direction because its chief organisations were so huge and immense that they were practically immovable. They argued that for practical purposes the Movement was ruled by an oligarchy beyond the reach of its members. In view of all of this, they considered that it was better to federate for specific purposes under imaginative and scientific control.

At the RACS Annual General Meeting in March 1937, there was another members' resolution included in the agenda, requesting that a communication be forwarded to the other three metropolitan societies urging that a Committee of Amalgamation be set up, after one or more of the other three societies had passed a resolution endorsing the principle of amalgamation. The General Committee took the view that there should be a committee of enquiry set up before such a proposal was considered, and pointed out that there was no guarantee of the present conditions of employment prevailing in an amalgamation. The Committee thought that the fusion of the Royal Arsenal and London societies was not the most desirable path – their dividend policies and political approach widely differed – and indicated that a merger with South Suburban Society would be of greater advantage to members. As a result, the members were advised to vote against the proposal, which was lost by 618 votes in favour and 2, 178 against.

The events leading up to the Second World War seemed to have taken the steam out of this activity, and the proposal was never seriously considered again, in spite of national activity generated by the Co-operative Independent Commission's Report of 1958, which led to the Co-operative Union producing its *National Amalgamation Survey* in 1960. This Survey proposed a reduction in the numbers of societies from 875 to 307 – but made no recommendation for the four London societies, which were considered to be large enough in their own right.

The four London Societies Stand at the
National Co-operative Exhibition, Crystal Palace, 1934

The 1960s and 1970s saw intermittent talks between London and Royal Arsenal and Royal Arsenal and South Suburban. Perhaps the most serious attempt took place in the second half of the 1970s when the Royal Arsenal Society agreed in talks with South Suburban to adopt a completely new name for a new society (a previous sticking point) and, more importantly, to terminate its full-time board in favour of a part-time committee. This latter change came into effect in 1978, but South Suburban decided not to proceed. A further approach was made in 1981 but again South Suburban decided to withdraw from the negotiations to form a South Eastern Society.

A single society for London was never achieved. London Society joined Co-operative Retail Services in January 1981, whilst South Suburban, Royal Arsenal, and Enfield joined the CWS in 1984, 1985 and 1992 respectively.

CHAPTER 10
CO-OPERATIVE ACTIVITY IN SOUTH LONDON DURING THE SECOND WORLD WAR

ROYAL ARSENAL CO-OPERATIVE SOCIETY

The various happenings of the six traumatic years from 1939 to 1945, despite the havoc and destruction caused by bombing, flying bombs and rockets, revealed a story of achievement, and illustrated that working together in the true spirit of co-operation overcame trading difficulties, mass evacuation and the hazards of aerial bombardment.

The Response to War
Problems began with the registration for rationed goods, and 400,000 South Londoners made themselves dependent on the RACS for food. The steady stream of men being called up into the armed services from the RACS – as many as a hundred a month – created service problems, but soon women were taking their place behind the counter, in dairy depots and on bakery rounds. Despite the bombing, milk and bread were always on the doorstep – bread delivered three days a week and the milkman could not let you have an extra pint, whatever the reason.

Practically every branch was damaged to a greater or lesser extent – many of them were hit twice or three times! Ten branches, nearly all in the London boroughs, were completely destroyed – from the Old Kent Road branch, through

Charlton branch

to New Cross, Bermondsey, Deptford, Charlton and North Woolwich. Commonwealth Buildings was the scene of 20 separate incidents, and there is little doubt that most, if not all, of these were directed at the adjacent Siemens Brothers' factory – a former German cable, telephone, lighting and marine business – but missed the target. Mitcham industrial site in south-west London did not escape – 14 buildings were damaged and two destroyed. Coal and dairy depots, funeral offices and houses on the Society's estates at Abbey Wood and Eltham all received the full weight of the attacks.

Bomb damage at Commonwealth Buildings

Food and materials were scarce. The Society's trade at the outbreak of war had reached a record £10 million but, following evacuation and distribution difficulties, the sales position became acute and business fell by £2 million in a year. As a result, economies had to be introduced and the dividend at one time dropped to six pence (2½p) in the pound. Taxation on the Society's undistributed profits rose from nearly £39,000 in 1939 to £128,000 four years later, with the rate of tax rising from 5s 6d (27½p) in the pound in 1939 to 10 shillings (50p) in the pound in 1946.

'Business as usual' became the slogan of the Society at the outbreak of war, and it was coined from *Together*, the Society's staff magazine, which celebrated its first anniversary with this leader:

> Although we are at war, the world had not yet come to an end. We still need food and drink, clothes and furniture, tobacco and face powder...shops and factories, and the sooner we realise it, the sooner shall we at home play our part in helping to end this beastly war which none of us wanted. Our slogan as a Society and as individuals must be 'Business as Usual'.

RACS Home Guard Unit

The magazine proved to be one of the strong links between the Society and its absent employees. It told servicemen how the Society was coping. Its contents were varied – humorous stories, cartoons, features on the work of various departments, Society personalities, photographs of ARP crews and the Society's Home Guard units, gardening, and snippets of news about the Society. As the war progressed, *Together* became more a troops' magazine – with tales from the front line attracting the censor's blue pencil on more than one occasion.

Another link with serving employees was a fund set up by subscriptions from employees and their friends to send parcels to the troops. It started in April 1940 and over £22,000 was collected. During the first nine months, parcels were sent monthly but, with rapidly increasing numbers, this period was extended to two monthly. Rationing made it impossible to provide reminders from home, and essentially the choice was between cigarettes and a postal order. Until 1943, parcels were sent from Woolwich to every place where the troops were serving, but, following packaging difficulties, a contract was made with the Pietermaritzburg Co-operative Society in Natal, South Africa, under which it agreed to send the parcels. Sweets, chocolates and dried fruit were sent out from Natal to a large proportion of serving troops. However, parcels could not be sent to prisoners of war, and ten shilling (50p) vouchers were given to relatives every three months to accompany Red Cross parcels.

RACS Guildswomen sorting garments knitted by C.W.G. members in South East London

During the hostilities, thousands of troops and Londoners lived in deep shelters. At first, there was just one shelter in south west London, and a group of co-operators, many of them Guildswomen, agreed to take over the catering. It was soon evident that one shelter was not enough for the thousands of men of all nationalities who were passing through London, and three further shelters at Stockwell, Clapham North and Clapham Common were opened. Apart from supplying the food, the RACS Balham branch also carried out the packing and distribution from the beginning to the end of the war. Over 200,000 were catered for in 12 months and, in January 1944, American troops were served for four months in the Stockwell shelter, with numbers varying from 500 to 1,000 each night. On the first public night, over 3,000 settled in the Stockwell shelter with numbers increasing each night. For more than four months, the Guildswomen were feeding 10,000 people. Lectures and film shows were given by the Education Committee and over 100 books were donated towards a library.

Assistance was given to many members who lost their homes through enemy action, to enable them to obtain their rights under the complicated provisions of the War Damage Acts.

In spite of all their tribulations, members contributed nearly £15,000 to funds to help distress in Europe, Russia, and China, and in 1941 the Society contributed to official funds for the relief of distress caused by air raids in its area.

Education Work

The first sirens brought to an end preparations for classes, concerts, conferences, films and exhibitions, all arranged under the auspices of the Education Committee. Black-out in the early days prohibited all forms of entertainment but, by the Autumn of 1939, 60 study groups were working with local Evening Institutes.

About 90 per cent of Junior Circles were closed for safety reasons, but contact was made on a monthly basis through *Our Circle*, a childrens' magazine published by the Co-operative Press. The Woodcraft Folk were helped with a similar scheme. However, members of the Junior Circles entered examinations, and the successful ones went to Rhyl or Windermere summer schools arranged by the Co-operative Union.

Before the war, there were arrangements for 100 technical classes covering most of the Society's activities and, in addition, 300 boys were spending several hours a week away from their grocery and butchery counters continuing their education. This was ruined by the war but, after some re-organisation, nearly 30 classes started up again.

The raids of 1941 caused all 53 classes in the Autumn Session to be cancelled, although later on 29 managed to meet in the afternoons and Sunday mornings. Some drama and choral groups reformed and met throughout the war.

Special conferences were held to outline the extent of the Societys' trading problems. Food films, with commentaries by Ministry of Food experts, illustrated how to make the most of the rationed foods available and discussed the problems of housewives.

Exhibitions were held depicting life in Russia and China and to mark the centenary of the establishment of Rochdale co-operation, scholarships were awarded for a short-term course at the Co-operative College hostel at Wilmslow, Cheshire. Perhaps the greatest set-back was the abandonment of the London production of the Centenary celebration pageant after members of most of the London societies attended rehearsals at the Stoll Cinema or the Scala Theatre throughout the black-out and flying bomb raids.

The Political Field

The Political Purposes Committee took the positive decision to carry on meeting despite all the difficulties, and consideration of new legislation and other important moves were often started in the meeting room but ended in the air-raid shelter. From the start, the Committee was aware of the restrictions that war would place on the Society and it made clear to the General Committee that there would be no opposition if the political grant was reduced. A cut of one third was made – thus the Society made savings, as well as keeping pace with political development.

Apart from routine meetings, the Committee planned 300 visits to Guilds, organised a 25,000 signature petition which pressed for the speedy implementation of the Beveridge Report and arranged 16 conferences dealing with important national affairs. Not only did the Political Purposes Committee meet, but reports from local Labour Parties revealed that the Society's representatives – which numbered nearly 150 – continued as far as possible. Representation was also maintained on the National Executive of the Labour Party, the London Labour Party, the Standing Joint Committee of Working Womens' Organisations – Mrs A A Trueman was elected Chairperson – and the London Labour Womens' Advisory Committee with Mrs Councillor E V Coyle as Chairperson. The Committee's Secretary, Mr W H Green JP, took over the Chairmanship of the Labour Party during the critical time of 1942.

At the General Election in 1945, each of the Committee nominees from the Parliamentary Panel – Mrs J Adamson, Mr H Berry, Mr J Reeves and Rt Hon H Morrison – secured election. Furthermore, 27 Labour members were returned out of 29 constituencies covered by the Society. From 177 nominees on the Local Government Panel, 133 were successful at the municipal elections in the same year, eight becoming mayors of their boroughs.

More than 3,000 RACS staff went to war. 167 were killed; 16 died in prisoner of war camps; and 47 employees lost their lives through the blitz.

SOUTH SUBURBAN CO-OPERATIVE SOCIETY

War, and the rumours of war, in 1937 brought to a halt the movement of the population south and this, coupled with a steady return to the North and the Midlands, gave trade in those areas a remarkable stimulus. The Society's report for 1938 revealed a loss of over 2,000 members to this exodus. The Tonbridge Society was taken over in January of that year, when it was reported that a site for a departmental store had been purchased – but the war put paid to that. 1938 and 1939 saw the Society introduce optical and travel services through the CWS. The policy of supporting CWS services had been established in 1931 with the introduction of a dental service.

War commenced in September 1939, the year that saw the Society's coming of age, but no celebration was possible. Whilst sales were beginning to recover, they were still well below those achieved in the previous year. Only six half yearly members' meetings were held – instead of 16 – and quarterly meetings ceased to be held from 1940.

Nearly 12,000 members left the Society during the first three months of the war and there was a discontinuance of supplies to 40 schools. Total sales in March 1940 showed a 2 per cent decrease.

Croydon and adjoining districts were classified by the London County Council as evacuation areas, and it was just as well, because almost the first bombs dropped in August 1940 fell on Croydon Airport. Much of the Battle of Britain was fought over the Society's area, with the aerodromes of Biggin Hill, Croydon and Kenley as prime targets.

South Suburban War Damage

Day and night air raids were frequent, and these had the effect of accelerating the deterioration in sales, in spite of nearly 300,000 registering with the Society for their regular requirements of sugar, butter and bacon.

Bomb Damage

Many of the Society's properties were slightly damaged at this early stage but, in the next three years, they suffered heavily; the Croydon area endured damage generally, Penge suffered a direct hit in 1940, whilst Norwood Road was severely damaged, and Bellingham was completely destroyed in 1941. However, to offset the effect of this destruction, new premises were acquired in Farnborough, Sutton, Lower Kingswood (in Surrey), Caterham Valley, Bromley, West Norwood and Worcester Park, which would provide a springboard for post-war development.

The Co-operative Funeral Furnishing Service (CWS) was introduced in 1942, but was not linked to the Death Benefit Scheme until 1950, when a Chapel of Repose was opened in Purley.

In the two years ending in 1943, trade improved although decreases were still being recorded in membership. A family ration card introduced by the Society helped to overcome dissatisfaction caused by shortages of supplies.

As in Royal Arsenal, the Society provided a useful social service by providing expert advice to its members to pursue their war damage claims and compensation.

The unmanned flying bomb (V1) atttacks commenced in June 1944, and Croydon was reported to have been the most bombed town, but other districts – Penge, Beckenham, Bromley, Mitcham, and Sydenham – suffered severely. A total of 140 Society premises were damaged, thousands were evacuated, a decrease of 33 per cent in bakery business was experienced, and the total loss of trade for the six months to September, 1944, was over £160,000. A report in *Home Magazine* reported that nearly 1,100 bombs fell and over 1,300 persons were killed in districts covered by the Society.

The flying bombs ceased in August 1944, only to be followed by the more powerful V2 rockets two months later. By the time these ceased in March 1945, many more lives had been lost, but the Society escaped further serious damage.

During the war, contact was made with as many of the staff serving in the forces as possible, with copies of the *Wheatsheaf* magazine and cigarettes regularly forwarded. Prisoners of war also received cigarettes, games, books, music and clothing. In 1943, the Society paid into the Auxiliary Pension Fund an amount equivalent to that which would have been contributed by employees.

Government Savings Weeks – Warships Week, Wings for Victory, Victory Week, Salute the Soldier, and Thanksgiving Week – were all supported with generous help from the CWS and CIS. In addition, a contribution was sent in 1944 to the Freedom Fund, an appeal launched by the International Co-operative Alliance (ICA), and aid sent to Russia and China when backed by members through quoting their share number on purchases.

War-time paper recycling in Croydon

September 1946 saw the greatest social gathering ever arranged by the Society, when 5,000 employees and friends attended a reunion which was held in the Royal Albert Hall, London, to welcome home all employees who had served in the forces or were engaged in the Civil Defence Services.

In the six years from 1939 to 1945, two grocery and four butchery branches were opened. The Society's sales increased from £4.6 million to £5 million, share capital from £3.1 million to £4.3 million, and membership from 199,000 to 212,000.

The outbreak of war brought all educational activities to a standstill. Guild meetings, conferences, classes and a few new junior groups were reported, but it was not until September 1945 that progress was recorded in re-establishing normal activities.

CHAPTER 11
THE RACS IN SOUTH LONDON, KENT AND SURREY: 1945 to 1985

Postwar Activities

The RACS could build only slowly after the end of the Second World War in 1945. Many of its shops and stores were damaged, and repairs were difficult to complete due to the shortage of materials, priority being given to heavy industry and the export trade. As a result, expansion was mainly achieved by the acquisition of existing businesses, 20 mainly small grocery shops with their licences and food rationing regulations being bought out. In addition, two hotels were purchased in 1945 and 1946 on the Isle of Wight, one in Sandown, the other in Shanklin. R Duval & Son, a coach operator

Savoy Hotel, Shanklin, I.O.W.

was acquired in 1946 and, in the following year, George Penn Ltd, a removal business with a small chain of cycle and radio shops was purchased; this was followed in 1949 by a small ice cream factory in Abbey Wood, south east London. New departments also began to appear around this time. A bookshop was opened in the Woolwich store in 1947, followed by a jewellery department two years later. Both were successful, and departments were opened in the Society's other departmental stores. Morden store in Surrey, partially opened in 1939, was finally opened completely in 1948, and two years later the Society acquired the department store of Holdrons in Balham. Brixton bakery re-opened in 1951 after reinstatement of its severe war damage suffered in the early part of the war. Where building did take place, this was achieved through the erection of temporary prefabricated buildings – supplemented by

Morden Store completed with upper floors, 1948

mobile shops – until a long-term building programme could be put into operation in the 1950s.

Following the retirement of F G (Fred) Burch in 1953, W J Morton was elected Secretary of the Society. Morton joined the Society in 1922 and had been previously the Society's Accountant and Assistant Secretary. Perhaps his most notable achievement was as architect and builder of the Society's credit services.

Retailing Revolution

Food rationing and controls continued until 1954, and this too had the effect of holding back recovery in trade and thereby bringing frustration to many experienced grocers, who decided to leave the industry and seek better wages and conditions in other trades. The loss of these experienced staff was counteracted by the introduction of self-service retailing from the USA, with its boost to sales and reduction in overheads. In addition, the employment of women that had begun during the war continued, and, as self-service developed, their numbers increased, with part-time employment taking over from full-time work. Yet, it was not until many years later that married and part-time women were able to join the Society's Superannuation Fund.

Woolwich department store bookshop, 1968

John Corina, a member of the Society's General Committee, visited the USA in 1947 to study this new method of retailing, and following his report the Society opened its first self-service grocery shop in Tooting, south west London. By the mid-1950s, the RACS had opened 30 such shops and this number had increased to 80 by the end of the decade. Many of these were corner shops of less than 1,000 square feet, which proved to be at a disadvantage as larger supermarkets developed. The latter provided a greater range of goods and secured economies of scale, thus making smaller stores uneconomic, eventually bringing about their demise or disposal.

These changing conditions affected consumer preferences, and the RACS quarterly report of June 1954 to its members commented that the steep rise in the cost of living since 1952 had now steadied and consumers were seeing some important reductions in prices. 'The price factor, widening of consumer choice and keener competition, together with cut prices being operated by some competitors all have an effect' in making increases in trade and profitability more difficult to achieve. To meet this competition, the Society carried out 'a policy of fair standards in price, quality and working conditions'. It also required a change in direction and some rationalisation. Woolwich laundry, situated in Commonwealth Buildings, was closed and the business passed on to the Kent Federal Society. The Preserve Factory in Abbey Wood, severely damaged during the war, was closed and supplies were taken from the CWS, whilst the decline in bread sales, brought about by the availability of alternative products, led to the closure of Brockley bakery.

Southwark Park Road, 1940

The Government rehousing programme initiated during these years saw many RACS members leave the area to settle in other parts. But the potential to recapture the loss of food business and move into more remunerative non-food businesses was attractive, particularly with the removal of credit restrictions in the early 1950s, which allowed more favourable hire purchase terms to be offered until they were re-imposed in 1956.

To meet this situation, the Society built, reconstructed or remodelled its stores at Chessington, Southwark Park Road, Blackfen, Welling, New Malden, Tolworth and Rye Lane, Peckham. These developments brought calls to members from the General Committee for increasing loyalty both in trade and capital. Recruitment campaigns were carried out, amongst which was the trade exhibition held on Woolwich Common in 1956 under the joint auspices of the Society and the CWS, officially opened by Lord Williams the CWS President, and attended by over 160,000 people.

The central problem of co-operative finance, i.e. the attraction, retention and accumulation of capital, was becoming more difficult to wrestle with both at local and national level – although, in the eyes of many societies, Royal Arsenal, with its formidable share capital base (in spite of instant withdrawability) and strong reserves, was looked upon as a 'Bank of England' society. However, these capital, and other, difficulties were considered by a special independent inquiry commission under the Chairmanship of the Right Hon Hugh Gaitskell MP, Leader of the Labour

Southwark Park Road reconstructed, 1955

89

Party. Its report, published in 1958, proposed a programme of regional mergers and the need to inject new capital into retail development to arrest the decline in co-operative trade, which had fallen nationally from 20 per cent at the end of the war to 12 per cent by 1957.

In all this upheaval it was vital that a continuity of policy should be followed, and this was in the minds of members of the RACS when they approved changes to the Society's rules, recommended by a Rules Revision Committee in 1954-1955, one of which was the extension of the period of office of statutory committees from two to three years.

The year 1958 marked the 90th anniversary of the formation of the RACS and to celebrate the occasion the Society arranged a varied programme of events in stores, members' competitions, special programmes for International Co-operative Day and a big campaign of publicity. Targets were set to reach £30 million sales and 400,000 members. In the two months of May and June, nearly 18,000 new members were made, the success of the venture being due to personal introductions made by employees, members of the auxiliaries and members of other organisations associated with the Society. Over 40 per cent of these new members made purchases with the Society, the average per person being nearly £37. Unfortunately, the sales target was not met, due to some extent to a bus strike which affected non-food sales, but more particularly to the abnormal trade recession, which reflected the acute troubles in the national economy. The *Home Magazine* – previously the CWS magazine *Wheatsheaf* – reported that the Economist Intelligence Unit had commented, 'The British economy is going through its roughest patch since the war. Production is down some 5 per cent below the

Bexleyheath departmental store, 1960

peak months of 1957. Industry as a whole is operating at about 80-85 per cent of capacity.'

The RACS continued to convert its grocery shops to self-service. New non-food stores at New Malden, Bexleyheath and Tolworth were opened; Rye Lane, Peckham and Welling were reconstructed; and a television rental scheme started.

Expansion

The 1960s were to see a considerable expansion in the Society's trading area brought about by mergers with nine societies throughout Kent and Surrey, due, no doubt, to the opinions expressed by the Independent Commission that it was desirable to reduce the number of retail societies to between 200 and 300 – the belief being that many were too small to provide all the necessary services.

However, before these changes came about William (Bill) Morton, the Society's Secretary, retired early on health grounds in 1960, having held the office for seven years. To take his place, the members elected Maurice J Cox, the Society's Assistant Secretary, who had been employed by the RACS man and boy. He was a chartered secretary and accountant. He had taken the leading role in keeping the Society in the forefront of financial and accounting techniques, e.g. changing the Society's 90 year old system of metal checks to record members purchases to the paper check system adopted by most societies in

RACS main frame computer

the UK, which required members to remember their membership numbers and quote them when required. He was also responsible for the installation of a mainframe computer, instituting new systems both within the RACS and in other societies. Along with Jim Walker, the Society's General Manager, Cox brought to fruition nine mergers with neighbouring societies in the period from 1962 to 1970.

The following year saw a change to the celebration of International Co-operative Day, which had been established for nearly 40 years. Traditionally, this first Saturday in July had been marked by holding outdoor events at Abbey Wood and Morden. Whilst these had been successful, times and conditions were changing, and it was decided to hold a week's programme of events, culminating in Co-operative Day, which would attract greater interest from the public in the Society's area and present the aims and principles of Co-operation more effectively. This initiative was applauded by Mr W P Watkins, BA, Director of the International Co-operative Alliance.

1962 was the year that the 5½ day, 41½ hour week for shop staff was introduced; that the Labour weekend newspaper The *Sunday Citizen* was launched; and that the CWS conducted the biggest nationwide publicity campaign ever undertaken by the Movement, with the theme 'Come Co-operative Shopping'.

However, the outstanding feature of the year for the RACS was the September merger with the Woking Co-operative Society. This Society had

Woking Society, Kingfield branch

been formed in 1899 by a group of trade unionists in the town under the guidance of the Guildford Co-operative Society. Business was started in Chertsey Road, Woking, followed by a further shop in Church Street three years later. In the five years ending with the outbreak of war in 1914, the Society, with its own labour, built 30 houses and a shop at Horsell. Further land was acquired and divided up, some plots being developed privately, and it was in 1935 that the estate was taken over by the town. The Surbiton Society ceased operations in 1912 and, during the following eight years, Woking Society opened four shops in that area. Similar developments by that Society also took place in the early 1920s in the Sunningdale and Camberley districts when the local societies ceased to trade.

In 1933, 14 square miles of Woking Society's territory, lying between the RACS south western boundary and Thames Ditton were transferred to the RACS and this resulted in the shops at Tolworth and Surbiton along with 1,600 Woking Society members being transferred to the RACS. The Society's registered office and new central store at Percy Street was opened in 1936, and it was probably the first co-operative society to operate a family medical aid scheme on the basis of an annual deduction from the dividend of members who joined the scheme. At the time of the merger with the RACS, the Woking Society had 10,000 members and an annual trade of over £630,000, which was achieved through its central premises and 12 branches from Claygate and Hersham in the west, Send in the south, Camberley in the west and Sunninghill in the north.

The severe weather conditions of 1963 made trading difficult. March of that year saw the changeover of television reception from the 405 to the 625 line system, providing improved picture definition; the co-ordination under one management of bakery services between the RACS and South Suburban Society; and the introduction by the RACS of the first co-operative laundromat in the south of England at Abbey Wood. The second merger with the Godalming and District Society became effective in July. This Society had started life in 1897 under the guidance of the Guildford Society and the enthusiasm of the local Liberal club. The Society conducted its annual trade of nearly £450,000 through its central premises at Bridge Street, Godalming, and four branches at Witley, Chiddingfold, Farncombe, and Elstead. At the end of the year, the

Abbey Wood laundromat, 1963

CWS celebrated its centenary, with members of the RACS visiting an exhibition in Manchester, travelling by special train organised by the London Society.

At the end of 1963, the Society's sales for the year achieved the record figure of £28 million, which represented an increase of £1.5 million on the previous year.

The Conservative Government's decision in 1964 to close down the Woolwich Arsenal struck at the heart of the RACS, which had been founded nearly 100 years before through the efforts of a group of workers employed there, and this early link had survived through each successive generation. A letter of protest was sent by the General Committee to the Minister of War, suggesting that the decision be reversed, and this was followed by a motion from the Political Purposes Committee to the Annual Conference of the London Labour Party – all to no avail.

On the trading scene, the growth of stamp trading and the Government's decision to introduce legislation banning resale price maintenance, coupled with further increases in expenses, made it essential that sales be expanded. Accordingly, the Society's development programme progressed vigorously, with new stores being built and others being modernised and redeveloped. The off-licence business expanded and the new businesses of in-store bakeries, laundries and dry-cleaning shops started.

September saw the end of an era with the announcement by the CWS that it was to discontinue the publication of the *Home Magazine* and replace it by a new publication under the title *Good Shopping*. The magazine was first published as *Comradeship* and changed its name in January 1962. Its local pages provided a vital link between members and the Society, spreading news of commercial and educational activities. The new publication took away the opportunity of RACS information being circulated in a national

93

Interior Upper Wickham Lane off licence, 1964

magazine and, following consultations with the CWS, it was decided to produce a local supplement under the masthead *News of the RACS* (renamed *RACS News*) with effect from December, 1964.

By the end of the year, sales had reached £29.5 million and dividend was 6d in the pound.

During 1965, the RACS continued to battle against large-scale competition in the food trades, particularly near to its main stores. This was met by the introduction of new techniques; the modernisation of its departmental stores at Woolwich, Lewisham and Tooting; increased administrative savings and improved management information achieved by the introduction of a new computer; and the continued up-dating of food shops to supermarkets.

The third society to merge with the RACS in July 1965 was the Haslemere and District Co-operative Society, which had its beginnings in 1903 in a small centre of rural population in Surrey. It started trading in grocery, provisions and bread-baking, and in two years had acquired its own bakery. The Society's central premises at Wey Hill, Haslemere, were opened in 1909 and extended 15 years later. In the two decades leading up to World War II, the Society expanded its trading base from Liphook, Hampshire, in the west to Petworth, Sussex, in the south and Beacon Hill in the north. In the period following the war, it joined neighbouring societies in the federal bakery, dairy and footwear repairing operations. At the time of the merger, the Society had an annual trade of nearly £460,000 and 6,000 members.

On the wider scene, the year was important for the Movement because it saw the publication of a plan by the CWS Joint Reorganisation Committee which aimed, 'To streamline buying and selling operations, lower prices for housewives, and win trade from the private supermarkets and chain stores.' To achieve this, it proposed a new relationship between retail societies and the CWS by the creation of 'a form

In-store bakery

of organisation which can co-ordinate the operations of the retail societies and the CWS.' The report, in addition to calling upon the 600 retail societies to agree to the CWS buying for all of them on a national scale, put forward the suggestion of a two-tier board structure – an elected part-time board responsible for policy-making and full-time appointed executives to carry it out. All the recommendations, except one of minor importance, were approved by substantial majorities.

Haslemere Society Wey Hill branch

The year came to a close with the General Committee's Report to members referring to the new regulations governing hire purchase and the fact that it was the first retailer in the country to announce reductions in prices of 'Hoover' products following the manufacturer's statement releasing retailers from price maintenance agreements. Members also considered and rejected a recommendation to hold members' meetings at half-yearly intervals instead of quarterly.

In achieving record sales of £31.2 million, which had been accomplished by cutting prices in food and non-food, the Society based its trading policy on three considerations:

- making good quality merchandise available at the lowest possible costs;
- providing good service, not only in shops, but in all the service departments;
- pressing ahead with the modernisation of shops and productive units.

Economic Problems

The last five years of the decade were marked by increasing Government indirect taxation, greater competition and a vast change in the Society's trading area. During this period, the Labour Government introduced, in 1966, the ill-conceived Selective Employment Tax (SET), which was designed to give manufacturers a relative advantage in costs compared with the service sector. Successive budgets imposed amongst other things: further increases in the rate of SET; a cut-back in Investment Allowances; increases in national insurance; a surcharge and an extension of the imposition of purchase tax; credit restrictions; the introduction of prescription charges; restriction on the provision of free milk to secondary schools; import levies; the imposition of the Land Betterment Levy as well as the usual increases in excise duties and road tax. Understandably, the public became very apprehensive about the future. In a business engaged in such a wide variety of trades in an unpredictable and erratic economic climate set by the pattern of Government action, sales trends became more difficult to gauge.

In addition to all of this, six new major supermarket competitors opened in the Society's area. This competition was met by the development and redeployment of existing shops to supermarkets, an extension of self-selection in non-foods, increasing mechanisation and the closure of uneconomic units. By 1967, six small dairy depots had been closed (whilst others had been enlarged and modified) along with 15 small food shops. These developments affected staff levels and 700 employees left the Society in six years.

The ending of Resale Price Maintenance on chocolate, sweets and cigarettes enabled substantial price cuts to be made, thus stimulating sales. This, coupled with the Society's continuing policy of modernisation of its food shops and the rapid expansion of its off-licence business, enabled it to hold its own in the food business.

Centenary and Mergers

In 1968 the full effects of devaluation were beginning to make themselves felt. A number of efforts were made to arrest the decrease in non-food trade brought about by Government restrictions. Joint promotions were run in conjunction with the CWS and the London Society; a series of fashion shows were held and over 3,000 attended; in conjunction with Hoover, a stand was taken at the Ideal Home Exhibition; special sales drives were arranged, and better merchandise values were offered through vigorous support of national co-operative marketing schemes.

1968 was also the year that the Society celebrated its centenary, and a whole series of activities were organised and arranged – overseas scholarships, the presentation of a china tea service to those with over 50 years' membership, special attractions and commemorative investment opportunities and various other functions. However, the year will be particularly remembered for the mergers with the Gravesend, Slough and Addlestone societies, which resulted in the Society's trading area being extended to 420 square miles.

The Borough of Gravesend Society in Kent was formed back in 1884, by river pilots and lightermen, in spite of strong opposition from traders in the town. Its first properties were located in Harmer Street, and it was not long before deliveries were commenced to Northfleet and Swanscombe. It was in 1917 that the Cliffe at Hoo Society, founded in 1889, joined Gravesend. The Society opened its new central premises in Harmer Street in 1932 and, two years later, whilst celebrating its Jubilee, started a bread pension scheme for qualifying members. Following active participation in federal milk, laundry and funeral operations, it opened a new furnishing, footwear and menswear store at Milton Road, in 1939. The Society changed its name to the Gravesend Co-operative Society in 1962 and, at the time of the merger with the RACS in May 1968, it had a 10 square mile trading area, centred in the town with boundaries formed by Chalk to the east, Greenhithe in the west and Meopham to the south. The Society was achieving sales of £2.6 million through departmental stores, grocery, meat and poultry shops, off-licences and specialist florist and photographic shops. It had nearly 30,000 members, who held share capital of over £380,000.

Gravesend Society, Cliffe-at-Hoo branch

The Slough and District Co-operative Society was established in rural Buckinghamshire in 1892, when it opened its first shop in the High Street. It was not until the end of the Second World War that expansion took place – and this occurred rapidly with the opening of 13 branches in an area of 25 square miles from Iver in the east, to Windsor in the south and Stoke Poges in the north. It was in July 1968 that the merger with the RACS became effective and, at that time, the Society had annual sales of £2.3 million achieved through a central store, rebuilt in 1962, specialist grocery and meat and poultry shops and a processing dairy.

In 1902, the Addlestone and District Industrial Co-operative Society opened a temporary shop on Alexander Road followed, in the same year, by its first branch premises in Station Road. The following year, an Education Committee was formed and in 1914 a merger with the Cobham Society took place. The Society merged with the RACS in September 1968, when it was

Slough Society Central Premises late 19th Century

operating in an area of 40 square miles in the County of Surrey bounded by Chertsey in the north, Ottershaw to the west, Cobham on the southern border and Walton eastwards. Its annual sales were £1.1 million, which were achieved through its departmental store in the town and food and

Addlestone Society Station Road branch circa 1900

non-food shops along with a number of hairdressing salons. Its membership of nearly 17,000 held approximately £300,000 share capital.

These three mergers were quickly followed in July of the following year by another. The Faversham Co-operative Society in Kent had been formed in 1874 and traded in various sites in and around the town. Eight years later, an Education Committee was elected and a fund commenced for its work. It changed its name to the Faversham and Thanet Co-operative Society following a merger with the Isle of Thanet Society in 1933 and, as a result, expanded its trading area to include the Kent resorts of Whitstable, Tankerton, Swalecliffe, Birchington, Westgate, Margate, Broadstairs and Ramsgate. Co-operative Congress was held at Margate on three occasions in 1939, 1952 and 1976. At the time of the merger with the RACS, the Society had annual sales of £1.3 million achieved through 19 branches, two departmental stores and a specialist non-food shop. It also operated a meat and poultry factory as well as dairy productive and distributive services.

Faversham Society shop interior

The decade ended with no change in the significant trends in consumer spending, with increases in food sales being partially offset by decreases in non-food. Sales per member were nearly £42 compared with £37.50 for the previous year. RACS trading policy continued to be to keep prices as low as possible. Joint food promotions with the London and South Suburban societies were undertaken supported by advertising covering the whole of London and the Home Counties. The number of Co-op own brand goods was expanding and supermarkets were stocking over 200 lines.

The 1970s saw radical changes to the pattern of trading brought about by increasing competition, inflation and government fiscal policy.

Superstores and Dividend Stamps

Shops were becoming larger, especially supermarkets and superstores. The RACS endeavoured to keep ahead of the situation and, in doing so, closed many small units, both food and non-food, in order to avoid tarnishing its trading image, putting its financial viability in jeopardy and risking its staff and recruitment programme. One of the reasons why the Movement lost a proportion of its trade in the 1950s and 1960s was, to quote the National Economic Development Office Report of 1971, 'Its main

difficulty had been in getting rid of the old rather than introducing the new.' In the first half of the 1970s, the Movement started to recover some of this lost ground by proceeding with its modernisation and rationalisation pogrammes at a faster rate. As far as the RACS was concerned, about 100 out of 170 food shops open in 1960 had been closed by the middle of the 1970s.

Dividend Stamp book

Along with changes to its trading profile, a controversial recommendation was submitted to members to change the traditional dividend system, and members approved, after some stormy meetings, the introduction of dividend stamps in September 1970. Whilst this was going on, the Sheerness and District Economical Co-operative Society merged with the Society.

Co-operation came early to the Isle of Sheppey with the launch of the Sheerness Economical and Industrial Cooperative Society in 1816. It was set up to supply bread, flour and fresh water to its members. In 1849, the Sheerness Cooperative Society was established for the sale of grocery and non-food items. The two societies amalgamated and became

Sheerness & District
Economical Co-operative Society, Ltd.
....
New Central Buildings.
92-100, High Street.

Central Premises Sheerness Society 1926

The Sheerness & District Economical Society in 1919, with a registered office situated at 100 High Street, Sheerness. Trading took place on the Isle of Sheppey through a central store, eight food shops, 12 non-food units, six specialist butchery shops and three off-licences. There were 220 employees. At the merger Sheerness Society had annual sales in excess of £1.1 million, 13,500 members and share capital of £230,000.

Dividend stamps stimulated a substantial increase in trade, helped no doubt by new stores and supermarkets being brought on stream and supported by out-of-town units where these could be justified and planning permission could be obtained. Economic factors were increasingly mitigating against small shop operations, and these were closed down where they had little or no hope of competing or where they could not be brought up to a modern standard.

During the first month of 1971, the Guildford and District Co-operative Society merged with the RACS. It was in 1891, with the help of the Reading

Guildford Society departmental store

Society, that the Guildford Society opened its first shop at Haydon Place, Guildford. In 1916, the Society was joined by the Leatherhead Society, followed by the Horsham Society in 1921, and the Dorking Society four years later. In 1935, a federal dairy was established with neighbouring societies and it traded as the Co-operative Federal Dairy Society, later changing its name to the Co-operative Dairy Society. The annual trade of the Guildford Society at the time of the merger with the RACS was £2.3 million. It had 42,000 members and 350 employees and traded in an area around Guildford stretching from Leatherhead in the north, to Dorking in the east and Partridge Green, Sussex, in the south.

The Government introduced Decimal Currency in February 1971, followed by a 50 per cent reduction in Selective Employment Tax. The change of currency had the effect of increasing prices, and a report in *The Times* on food prices after decimalisation commented, 'In the five months since the end of February, the Co-op stores, in our sample, had by far the best record, showing increases of just 5 per cent, a full percentage point below the all-stores average.' This provided some evidence of the steps taken by the Movement as a whole to keep prices down, which was also helped by a reduction in purchase tax on a wide range of merchandise.

Decimal Currency Training

The retailing scene was one of price cutting in food, whilst non-food competition was met by intensive promotional activity in conjunction with CWS and the other metropolitan societies. Some indication of this activity can be judged from the General Committee's Report to Members of December 1972. 'The question of inflation and rising prices is constantly the concern of the Society and, although the Government's 90-day freeze on prices covers a wide range of goods and services, it still leaves the price of many important items subject to day to day market fluctuations.' The volatile nature of food markets at that time was demonstrated by 159 changes in the price of sugar for the year 1972.

Senior Management Changes

The 1960s and 1970s also saw the Movement moving away from the traditional dual senior management positions of General Manager and Secretary to the appointment of a Chief Executive Officer, with overall responsibility for both roles.

In November 1972, Maurice Cox, the Society's Secretary for the previous 12 years decided to retire after completing 48 years' service with the Society. In keeping with the national trend, the General Committee appointed Jim

Ron Roffey RACS Secretary

Walker, the Society's General Manager as Chief Executive, the first official in the RACS to hold the title since 1937. In his new role, Walker took under his wing the additional responsibilities of finance and accounting, with the Financial Controller reporting to him rather than the Secretary as in the past. In Cox's place, the Committee recommended the appointment of Ron Roffey, the Society's Assistant Financial Controller as Secretary of the Society, to the members, and they agreed.

Roffey, a local man, was a product of the Societys staff training scheme. He joined the Society's Central Office staff in 1950, after completing his national service in the Royal Air Force. Following a course of study, he was awarded one of the Society's Diamond Jubilee Scholarships in 1954, tenable at the Co-operative College, Loughborough, and, after two years full-time study, completed the Co-operative Secretaries' Diploma. He returned to Powis Street, and in 1959 was promoted to senior clerk in the Accountant's office, and by 1960 he was Assistant Accountant and eleven years later Assistant Financial Controller.

It is interesting to note that, in spite of the Secretary's reduced financial and administrative responsibilities under the new arrangements, the integrity, honesty and reputation of the office that had been built up in the past continued. Roffey sat in the Board Room as the members' elected representative and held the delicate balance of responsibility to the General Committee on one hand, and to the Chief Executive on the other. The Society's rules were not amended to any great degree to take account of the changed situation; e.g. under rule, the Secretary was an officer (being elected by the members), and, apart from gross misconduct, could only be removed from office by a meeting of members; furthermore, Committee Meetings could not proceed without his presence. This authority was not extended to the Chief Executive. It is to the credit of both officials that this unusual situation did not create difficulties, and Roffey's increasing popularity and the respect in which he was held by both members and staff in the ensuing years were to play a significant part in the successful conclusion of the 1985 merger with CWS.

The Society's greatly enlarged area brought about changes to its structure of representation and lines of communication from members to the central adminstration. The Education Committee's electoral districts were reduced from ten to three and its number of elected members from 24 to 15. A number of District Committees were formed, made up of former management committees of the merged societies with the objective of maintaining local contact and securing knowledge and expertise in helping to preserve, develop and extend co-operative interests in their areas.

In an endeavour to take steps to improve members' participation, a special committee was set up to explore the subject and, as a result of meetings held with the Education and Political Purposes Committees and the Members' Council to discuss a document *The Encouragement of Member Participation*, the principle of quadrennial elections for the Society's three main committees was recommended. Also recommended were a four-year term of office, with voting in polling stations taking place each alternate year; a reduction in quorum from 30 to 20 for members' meetings, and the introduction of the Kent Joint Co-operative Council for a trial of three years with effect from June 1975. These recommendations were subsequently approved by the members.

In the event, the latter experiment of bringing together representatives of the General, Education and Political Purposes Committees along with the Chairman and Secretary of each of the Education Councils in the County in order to make representations to the General Committee on trading activities and developments (thus securing the Society's educational and political objectives as well acting as a means of communication between the members and the standing committees), was so successful that similar councils were set up later for the London and Western areas.

By the middle of the decade, food price inflation was running at 25 per cent and difficulties were being experienced in obtaining supplies. The four metropolitan co-operative societies worked closely together in both food and non-food promotions and used television and the London evening press for advertising. Their total trade for 1975 was approximately £300 million and together they controlled 50 department stores, 800 food branches and nearly 2,000 dairy rounds. It was at about this time that a Co-operative Union National Federation Special Committee was reporting on the desirability of creating a single federation to replace the Co-operative Union and the Co-operative Wholesale Society, but once again radical thinking did not bring about change.

The beginning of the second half of the 1970s saw the Society's turnover reach £100 million, although the spending power of the average customer was declining in spite of a falling rate of inflation. It was about this time that discussions were taking place with neighbouring societies – but principally with South Suburban – on the possibility of setting up a regional society under the Co-operative Union's Regional Plan 2. However, it was clear that, before any meaningful discussions could take place, Royal Arsenal would have to adopt a part-time voluntary committee in place of its full-time Board, falling into line with other regional societies in the UK.

After long discussions in the Boardroom, a proposal to this effect was submitted to the members in March 1976. Following well attended meetings, members agreed that with effect from March 1978 the full-time committee of seven members be replaced by a part-time committee of 12, to be elected for a four-year term of office over the whole of the Society's area

RACS's New Part-time General Committee and Officials 1980

Back Row:
A. J. Oberman; R. A. Balfe; W. N. Farrell; R. A. Roffey (Secretary); J. H. Walker (CEO);
T. G. Lewis (CEO Designate); N. L. Halsey; A. E. Norris; C. S. Raggett; C. S. Shrive

Front Row:
F. W. Styles; Ms S. M. Day; G. F. Hunn (Chairman); Mrs I. L. Handley; C. C. Job

under the proportional representation system of voting. On the basis of favourable and positive discussions between officers of both societies, it was thought at Royal Arsenal that its members' decisions would open the door for a merger, but South Suburban decided not to proceed.

The trading scene continued to be difficult with cut prices, supply difficulties and increasing expenses. The volume of retail trade recorded for 1976 was the lowest for three years. In South London, particularly the boroughs of Southwark, Lewisham and Greenwich, there was a continual fall in population and jobs and this, coupled with a national policy to encourage employers to move out of London, had a considerable effect on the Society's business. Prices tended to drift upwards, but the Society continued to operate a cut-price policy under a 'Cuts that Count' campaign with a consequent loss of gross margin.

In spite of a sharp drop in national volume sales for 1977, a situation that was greatly influenced by the recession in world trade, cautious Government economic policies and high rates of unemployment, RACS sales reached nearly £124 millions helped in part by the opening, in October, of its first superstore at Westwood near Broadstairs in Kent. The Society was still operating a large number of small food shops – but a number of these had to be closed in view of the declining population and their inability to attract staff and be operated profitably. Difficulties of supply and quality of certain merchandise were further aggravated by the decision of RACS members, supported by Co-operative Congress, to cease to sell any South African goods, as a protest against its racialist policies.

Member Involvement

Reports to RACS members in the latter years of the 1970s frequently included the convening of special general meetings to consider a number of constitutional matters. Apart from the major change in 1978 from a full-time to a part-time Board, perhaps the most important other changes were the termination of the Halls Fund Committee in 1980, and the reorganisation and linking of Education Councils and Joint Co-operative Councils with the Members' Council at local, district and central levels in a co-ordinated manner. The subject was discussed at some length at joint meetings of all the involved parties and led to the formulation of Area Members' Councils, which were open to any member of the Society, to consider local aspects of the Society's affairs of a trading, social, cultural, educational or political nature. They would be supplemented by District Members' Councils, operating in each of the three districts used for representation of the Education Committee, membership of which came from the Society's standing committees and each Area Members' Council in the district; and by a Central Members' Council which consisted of all members of the four standing committees and representatives appointed by, and from, each Area Members' Council.

The Central Members' Council mandated the Society's delegates to Co-operative Congress and CWS meetings, and it recommended candidates to the General Committee for elections to the CWS Board and the Sectional Board of the Co-operative Union. It also made recommendations to the Political Purposes Committee on how the Society's votes should be cast at national conferences of the Co-operative Party and Labour Party, for elected members to serve as Society representatives on general management committees of Constituency Labour Parties, and for co-operators to serve on local governing bodies and on the Parliamentary Panel of the Society.

The end of the decade saw the RACS holding discussions with the Co-operative Union and other societies in the south-east area with the objective of forming one regional South East Society covering South London,

Artist's impression – Woking superstore

Addlestone superstore 1974

Kent and Surrey but, in spite of goodwill between the individual societies, no progress was made. However, for marketing purposes, the metropolitan societies' group was joined by the Portsea Island and Brighton societies and, at that time, the group accounted for about 20 per cent of the country's co-op food trade whilst in non-food the 12 largest societies in the country had banded together for the purchase of mens' and womens' outerwear. In the bakery business, an agreement was reached with the Kent Federal Society, for it to take over the existing trade of the RACS, South Suburban and Invicta Societies, thereby making more efficient use of co-operative capital and ensuring support of the local federal society.

The first two years of the 1980s saw the economy continuing to contract at a rate of almost 2 per cent a year, with little sign of the recession bottoming out. This created an air of uncertainty, which was not helped by increasing unemployment (it had reached nearly three millions by the end of 1981) and high interest rates, causing consumers to think carefully about cash and credit commitments. These factors and intensive price competition prompted the Society to embark on further rationalisation programmes. Nearly 60 small food shops and four department stores were closed, and dividend stamps ceased to be given on food, fuel and dairy sales in 1981. These changes were followed by the closure of the food and fruit and vegetable warehouses (supplies being drawn from the CWS Regional Distribution Centre at Croydon), the merging of the computer operations with the CWS, and the slimming down of the central adminstration and other services.

But it was not all contraction. The larger Pricefighter supermarkets were refitted, Woking and Addlestone superstores came on stream, and a number of marketing schemes were introduced to stimulate non-food sales. Perhaps the most forward-looking decision taken during these two years was the Society's commitment to work with the South Suburban Society towards the establishment of a completely new South Eastern Co-operative Society but, once again, history was to repeat itself. After successfully completing most of the negotiations, including the completion of a rule book for the new society, it was announced in the RACS annual report for January 1982 that, 'the South Suburban Society had decided to withdraw from the present negotiations.' The 'love/hate' relationship continued. It was also at this time that moves were taking place for an early merger between the CWS and the Co-operative Retail Services (CRS), but these also were abortive.

Declining Fortunes

Active members of the RACS were expressing their concern with the decline in the fortunes of the Society. A Special Committee was set up to consider the implementation of greater member participation in the Society and the strengthening of democratic control. The Committee submitted its report in stages during 1981 and 1982, and this resulted in a decrease in the number of quarterly members' meetings which were spread over five days instead of three, with the extensive use of free transport to meetings (only to be discontinued in 1983), the introduction of money-off vouchers and a free prize draw for those attending – all in an effort to stimulate attendances.

Jim Walker, OBE, retired in 1981, after completing 45 years' service with the Society. The General Committee appointed T Granville Lewis, the Society's Non-Food Controller, as Chief Executive, a position he held for two years before leaving the Society. John Owen, the Society's Financial Controller, became Deputy Chief Executive and Financial Controller, a position he held until the merger with the CWS in February, 1985.

The difficulties being experienced by the Society since the mid-1970s were graphically outlined in a letter to the General Committee from the Society's auditors, Messrs Appleby and Wood, when reporting on the Society's results for the year ended January, 1982. Whilst acknowledging 'the considerable remedial and corrective action' that had been taken, they drew attention to the fact that the Society had last made a profit in 1977, and the accumulated deficit for the following five years was in excess of £17 million. In addition, the Society's overall financial position had been relieved by making profit of nearly £14 million on the sale of assets, and releasing over £3 million from the dividend stamp liability and deferred taxation. The auditors also drew attention to the deterioration in liquidity accompanied by a fall in share capital of £1.6 million.

A factor affecting the fall in liquidity not highlighted by the auditors was the decision of the Trustees of the Employees' Superannuation Fund to invest pension fund monies outside the Society, thus depriving it of a significant amount of cheap capital for investment in the business. This process was initiated by Maurice Cox, Secretary of the Fund, in the mid-1960s, and was accelerated by Ron Roffey following his appointment, due to increased political activity in the pensions field in the 1970s, aimed in part at reducing or eradicating self-investment of pension monies in parent organisations. Some idea of the loss of capital for inward investment can be obtained by the respective values of the Fund in 1972 and at the merger with the CWS in 1985. In 1972 the total value of the Fund was £5.1 million, of which £4.5 million was invested in the Society and secured by an equitable mortgage on a number of the Society's prime freehold properties. In 1985, the total fund stood at £23 million, all of which was invested in property and quoted investments outside the Society.

The relaxation of hire purchase controls came into effect in 1983, but this mainly affected areas of business outside the Society's trading orbit. Relatively high unemployment still existed in the Society's area, and it continued to operate a very aggressive food price policy in order to maintain its share of this business. The expected upturn in the economy – brought about by increased tax allowances and the clawback in mortgage interest rate tax relief offset by higher national insurance contributions – did not materialise, and the Society's trading increase did not reach that recorded in the Co-operative Union All Items Price Index. Further rationalisation resulted. Following shop closures, the Construction and Transport Divisions were drastically rationalised, and discussions started with the CWS and South Suburban Society on the merger of the dairy processing operation with the Kent Co-operative Society (this eventually came about in April 1984). The year saw merger talks taking place between South Suburban and Invicta Society, based in Dartford, with the RACS reiterating its support for the formulation of a strong independent South Eastern Society but, once again, there was no positive outcome.

The Future – An Independent View
It was towards the end of 1983 that the RACS decided to commission a report from an independent firm of management consultants on the future of the Society. Reports from Messrs Thomson McLintock Associates and the Society's management team were considered by the General Committee in March, 1984. These reports confirmed that many of the problems facing the Society were the same as those confronting other retail societies throughout the country, many of which arose from the failure of the Movement to organise itself better to compete in the current trading environment. However, it was considered that the Society had an independent future provided radical steps were undertaken to improve the overall trading performance. The Committee recognised the need for improvement and agreed to strengthen the food and non-food management structure. New food units with a viable future were decorated, refixtured and provided with new refrigeration. Capital was put aside to improve the Society's trading image and expand the sphere of operations wherever reasonable opportunities presented themselves. All sectors of the business were scrutinised to make them more cost effective, and unprofitable operations were sold.

Positive action was taken, although some aspects of the programme were held up, waiting for decisions to be taken by the General Committee which was due for re-election in May, 1984. Satisfactory increases in turnover were achieved, conversions undertaken and unprofitable operations disposed of. Whilst turnover increases were obtained and costs reduced, it was clear that improvements would not be made fast enough to put the Society on the improved financial footing that was required.

External forces were also taking a hand. Interest rates rose, and this brought about increased costs and a reduction in spending power. Whilst a marked improvement in profitability was achieved, it was still below the budgeted forecasts.

Co-operative market share in the South East had been declining for a number of years due to the rapid expansion of the major multiples and, to reverse this trend, the Society had sought without success the support of neighbouring societies to form a larger regional society. Thus, when the South Suburban Society merged with the CWS in July 1984, this objective became more difficult to achieve, especially as Invicta Society, which had been in unsuccessful merger talks with South Suburban, was concerned with the position of the RACS. This change in the retail pattern of South London was reviewed by the Society and its independent advisors, and the view was taken that to secure the interests of members, employees and retired employees, the Society should make application to the CWS to join the larger co-operative grouping in order to revitalise co-operative trade in the South East. Accordingly, the General Committee decided that the Chairman and Secretary should open negotiations with the CWS with a view to a merger. The CWS Board approved the application and the RACS set in motion the legal procedure that would bring about the fusion.

The Merger – Technical Difficulties

The procedure for a merger of two retail co-operative societies under the Industrial and Provident Societies Act necessitates two Special General Meetings being held by the transferor society, the first requiring its members to approve the merger by adopting a special resolution with a two thirds majority, and the second to confirm the earlier decision (if it is approved) by a simple majority.

The special resolution to be adopted provides amongst other things, for a straight exchange of share capital from one society to the other. Shares in retail societies are withdrawable and usually have a nominal value of £1 each, although this sum need not be paid up in full. Share capital can be held by an individual or jointly by two or more persons and this implies membership. Members are, in relation to the outside world, the Society. Shares confer voting rights and allow members to attend business meetings. Members also have, in the event of a winding up, liability limited to the amount of share capital they agreed to take up.

However, when retail societies merged with the CWS, they had to adopt a different special resolution, approved by the Registrar of Friendly Societies, which required members of the incoming society to be credited with one 10p with the balance being held in CWS loan capital. This variation was necessary because CWS shares were transferable and not withdrawable, a legal requirement to permit it to carry on the business of banking. It should be noted at this juncture that loan holders are not members of the society;

they are preferential creditors and have the legal right to have their debt paid to them before members receive a penny of their share capital.

As RACS members had nearly £6 million of individual share capital invested in the Society, the CWS took the view that this large sum should be preserved within the Movement to provide a flexible capital structure to maintain and expand individual share holdings as co-operative trading developed in the South East. To achieve this objective, it was decided to adopt the usual terms of merger which provided for a straight exchange of share capital. Individual RACS members would receive shares in the CWS equivalent to their shares in the RACS. The CWS Board had discretion within CWS rules to repay individual members' capital and, although CWS shares were not withdrawable, it was considered that this discretionary power to repay was sufficiently wide to allow for the usual resolution to be put to RACS members. The Registrar of Friendly Societies was informed of this proposal and, at the time of calling the first Special General Meeting, there had been no indication that the resolution presented any difficulty.

The special resolution was put to a series of 13 Special General Meetings of RACS members between the 10th and 14th December 1984, and was approved by 1254 votes in favour and 23 against.

On the 18th December, the Registrar confirmed to the CWS that, in view of the number of legal matters that still had to be resolved, it would be imprudent to pass the special resolution in the form adopted. However, the special resolution had already been approved. In spite of this, the Registrar ruled that RACS members must approve a resolution along the lines of that previously adopted by societies which had transferred engagements to the CWS. Accordingly, two Special General Meetings of RACS members were held from 7th to 11th January 1985. The first recommended members not to confirm the resolution agreed on 10th to 14th December, and the second requested members to agree the terms of the revised special resolution. The revised proposal was approved by 458 votes in favour with 10 against.

The decision was endorsed at a confimatory Special General Meeting held on 28th January to 1st February, 1985, by 447 votes in favour and 5 against, and the merger became effective on the 9th February 1985. At that time the RACS had a turnover of £156 million, share capital of nearly £6 million held by 296,000 members and reserves of £5 million.

Following the merger, discussions continued between the CWS and the Registrar to clarify the position for the future, and, at a CWS Special General Meeting in May 1986, a partial amendment of rules was approved, which designated CWS Share Capital as corporate shares and individual shares giving the CWS Board authority to determine withdrawability. Thus, independent retail societies which merged with the CWS after that date were able to adopt the special resolution, which provided members with shares in the CWS equal in value to those held in their own society.

CHAPTER 12
SOUTH SUBURBAN
CO-OPERATIVE SOCIETY:
1945 to 1984

Postwar Activities

The end of the Second World War saw employees returning to their jobs with the Society, to find retailing methods and practices had changed during their absence. As a fitting tribute to those who made the supreme sacrifice, a 13-acre sports ground and pavilion were purchased at Elmers End, Beckenham, in May 1947.

In its September 1945 half-yearly report to members, the South Suburban Society Board reported sales of £5 million, share capital of £4.3 million and a one shilling (5p) dividend. By the end of the decade, sales had almost doubled, but share capital and the dividend rate had remained static.

Trading development was mainly restricted to the acquisition of existing businesses because the priority for the granting of Ministry of Works licences was being given to housing which had suffered badly during the war. Over 70 trading units were opened in the five years following the end of hostilities, and these ranged over food and non-food departments. This period of rapid expansion saw the opening of the Society's 100th grocery shop at Stafford Road, Wallington, in December 1947, the purchase of a 20,000 square foot factory at Peall Road, Croydon, and the launch of the first self-service grocery shop at Bellingham in 1949.

Beckenham Sports Pavilion, 1956

In response to a Government request to the National Co-operative Authority to take steps to reduce potential inflationary tendencies in the economy, the Society, along with others, reduced the price of sugar, bacon, margarine, cheese, butter, preserves and bread in 1948. But this policy seriously affected the amount of profit for disposal. To enable members to get the benefit of co-op trading when on holiday or away from their home town, a National Membership Scheme came into operation in January 1949. Most societies joined the scheme which, it was hoped, would encourage trade and promote a sense amongst members of being part of a national movement. This scheme faded away in the 1960s with the introduction of dividend stamps.

This period also saw a considerable effort by employees to seek representation on the Board, a move that was consistently opposed by the Society as not being in its best interest. After a number of requisitioned meetings which failed to secure the necessary majority, the proposal was finally approved in May 1949. It was in the previous year that it was decided to set up Joint Advisory Councils with the objective of providing management with the opportunity to explain policy and development to staff, and to enable them to make a contribution to these processes.

The progress of the Society during the early 1950s showed promise and, by 1953, sales had reached nearly £13 million, which in part was due to increased prices, with resultant loss of gross profit. At that time food sales were over 80 per cent of the Society's total business. Dividend fluctuated between nine pence and ten pence (in old money) in the pound.

SSCS Bellingham branch

It was during 1952 that a freehold site adjacent to the Society's central premises in London Road, Croydon, was purchased, expanding a total frontage to 400 feet on the main road with over 270 feet on the return in Montague Road. This acquisition enabled shopping to be developed, the grocery warehouse enlarged and an additional exit provided at the rear of the site. The Randlesdown Road, Bellingham branch – destroyed by enemy action in May 1941, and already rebuilt as a self-service operation – was extended by the purchase of an adjacent shop to provide a butchery service. In the five years to 1952, the Society opened 100 new shops, and it also modernised the bakery, dairy, garage, and works departments along with transport replacements at a total cost of £1 million. Staff were provided with protective clothing, and members received full benefit under the provisions of the Society's Death Benefit Scheme, where funerals were carried out by the Co-operative Funeral Service.

Declining Fortunes

By 1954, increases in sales had slowed to single figures. Recession in some food trades and in textiles was brought about by price fluctuations, the complete decontrol of foodstuffs, the de-rationing of commodities, and the decline in bread consumption. By 1957, decreases in sales and share capital started to be recorded. The Board expressed its concern to members in its September 1957 report as follows:

> The rate of achievement is directly related to the extent to which a proper co-operative spirit can be developed; progress will be gravely impeded if personal interests are not subordinated to the greater interests of the Society.

The report went on to outline the steps being taken, warning that changes would have to take place in the existing organisation and administration, 'to ensure the future progress and prosperity of the Society.' Part of this programme was a survey undertaken by the CWS of the Society's properties to establish the extent of repairs and maintenance required. The cost of this work was met by reducing the dividend rate by one penny in the pound.

Competition was increasing. This was met by lower prices in a selected range of commodities, special offers, advertising and the provision of additional services. Bus, transport and dock workers' strikes in the summer of 1958 created further difficulties and, in order to maintain the dividend, which had fallen to three pence in the pound in 1960, withdrawals were made from reserves.

During these difficult years, considerable effort was made to increase the Society's efficiency and range of up-to-date services. Counter service grocery shops were converted to self-service; non-food operations were changed to self selection on an open store basis; new butchery, as well as fruit and vegetable shops were opened; shop fronts were replaced; and a new

SSCS Orpington branch, 1956

mechanical check office was opened in Bromley. New shops were opened at St Mary Cray, Hamsey Green, Worcester Park, Brixton, Norbury, Tattenham Corner, Orpington and Sevenoaks; and a new dairy was set up in Brixton. The process culminated in 1960 with the first stage in the modernisation of the Croydon store.

The Society's fortunes did not improve during the early 1960s. Sales along with share capital – which was at its lowest point since 1943 – continued to decline. Dividend at three pence in the pound was being maintained by utilising tax allowances and withdrawing from reserves. A Special Committee on member relations reporting in 1961 took the view that the Society's problems stemmed from three main sources: (a) failure to keep pace with retail development; (b) low morale of members and staff; and (c) the failure of management to build confidence amongst members and staff in its future plans. The Committee offered a variety of solutions. On the trading side, it proposed the disposal of small shops where appropriate and the conversion of others to self-service, for at that time, the Society was operating over 150 grocery shops, the bulk of which were counter service units. It also proposed the modernisation of larger units; selling some commodities at or below cost; giving dividend on grocery sales by way of vouchers redeemable in dry goods departments in areas of intense competition; undertaking research into new fields of consumer expenditure; and improving publicity and labelling and introducing Consumer Information Desks in larger stores.

On the subject of member participation, it proposed to substitute half-yearly for quarterly members' meetings, making them more attractive by improving venues and making use of exhibition materials, films, visual aids and fashion parades.

As far as management structures were concerned, it was proposed that the Management Committee be increased to 15 members and specialist sub-committees be set up with the Management Committee appointing members to the Society's subsidiary committees. The Special Committee's recommendations were approved in January 1962 and, as a result, a frantic programme of shop closures, self-service conversions and shop modernisations and refittings commenced. By 1965, 14 shops had been closed, 30 modernised and 135 grocery shops converted to self-service arrangements, which included the extensive modernisation of Penge to mark the 25th anniversary of its opening in 1938. It was in 1962 that the fruit and vegetable department was merged into grocery, and the centralised buying system abandoned. That same year saw the Society take over the responsibilities of the employees' sports club and pavilion at Elmers End, Beckenham.

In 1964 the Society lost the services of G A Preston, General Manager, after five years service. The Secretary, G E Warren, was appointed Administrative Officer, and three years later became Chief Executive Officer and Secretary.

The modernisation of trading premises coupled with the operation of a keen price policy in selected grocery branches and rising prices arrested the sales decline and, from 1963, the Society managed to maintain the dividend rate, but only by the sale of assets and withdrawals from reserve. This scenario continued until 1967, and during this four year period, the Society experienced increasing difficulty in making a trading profit and securing liquid capital for development. The main problem was the rapid escalation of expenses (many of which were outside the Society's control): annual wage awards, national insurance, increased duty on petrol, road tax, licences and insurance, and redundancy costs. The Society worked with its neighbour RACS to reduce costs, the latter taking over the management of the bakery department in 1963, followed by the check office and grocery warehouse accounting in 1966. To increase efficiency, management consultants were engaged, initially to review the processing dairy, and their task was later extended to advise on the trading management structure and the re-organisation of the transport fleet.

G. E. Warren
SSCS Chief Executive Officer

The Labour Government's imposition of the Selective Employment Tax in April 1966 brought about the closure of more uneconomic shops. The Society joined national and local protests to the Government to no avail.

In July of that year, the Board decided, after considering a marginal sales increase and a trading loss, that it was not prepared to use reserves to maintain the dividend. In spite of the extremely poor food trade, the Society continued its modernisation programme. In-store bakeries were being developed, notwithstanding a national decline in bread consumption.

A Special General Meeting in January 1967 authorised the Society to extend its capital raising powers and approved the transfer of £100,000 from the General Reserve Fund to the Dividend Equalisation Fund.

The annual accounts for the year ended January 1967 revealed a large trading deficit coupled with an overdraft for the majority of the year. The report to members also contained a Policy Report which detailed the consultations that had taken place with the Co-operative Union and the CWS on the advisability of a merger with the RACS. A long and thorough investigation had taken place – almost two years – and it was decided not to proceed. The Board expressed its confidence in the stability and potential of the Society but was mindful of the continuous withdrawal of members' capital during the previous 12 years, which had accentuated the need to raise liquid capital for development. To resolve these problems it was decided to adopt sale and lease-back arrangements in connection with a small number of properties to provide approximately £1 million, this being in addition to funds derived from unwanted and uneconomic assets and the institution of modern management controls.

SOUTH SUBURBAN BRANCHES

Widmore Road Bromley departmental store

Croydon Butchery self service, 1956

Hamsey Green Fruit & Vegetable Shop, 1954

Grove Park branch, 1955

Green Lane, Thornton Heath branch, 1967

Penge departmental store, 1938

Dividend Stamps – A Trading Stimulus

One of the actions taken to control costs was to review the very expensive method of recording members' purchases for dividend, collating them and, each half year, notifying every member of their purchases and dividend due.

A scheme was devised to replace this which was based upon the issue of dividend stamps for every purchase, stamp books being honoured as they were filled by cash, goods or transfer to members share capital. The proposal had the advantage of dispensing with the current expensive method of recording dividend, whilst at the same time removing the bias against non-members. The change was strongly opposed and rejected by members. However it was re-submitted and accepted. In the event it was so very successful that within weeks of its launch, the CWS sought permission to develop the scheme nationally, to avoid the proliferation of individual schemes. Thus the CWS Dividend Stamp Scheme was born. As a result, the Society's sales improved, the decrease in membership was relieved, and withdrawal of share capital fell substantially.

The annual accounts for 1968 – the year in which George Warren was appointed Chief Executive Officer and Secretary – revealed a loss of nearly £120,000, with over £440,000 being released from outside investments. This 50th anniversary year also saw the cessation of the Pharmacy department, the dramatic reduction of the Works/Maintenance department, the transfer of the Bakery department to CWS, with its Management Retail Services arm being engaged to overhaul the Society's dry goods function. Fully computerised share accounts for the Society's 241,875 members were produced through the RACS computer, and share capital stood at £2.5 million.

Cautious optimism was reported in the Committee's report for July 1968. Sales had increased by nearly 20 per cent, the highest figure recorded for the summer period for over 10 years. The Committee reported that, '(For the) first time for some years that the Society was able to pay its dividend out of profits without recourse to reserves.' Re-organisation continued. A completely new management structure was introduced and restrictions were made to the Death Benefit Scheme in the light of improved Social Insurance provision.

The next two years saw sales increase to nearly £17 million due to the popularity of dividend stamps, new shop developments, and the ending of Retail Price Maintenance on cigarettes. Whilst trading profit was the highest it had been for five years, increases in wages and Selective Employment Tax – the equivalent to 3d dividend – coupled with mounting losses due to burglaries, leakage and pilferage were continuing problems. In spite of this improved position, the introduction of new mechandising techniques, and modernisation of credit services, the Society was still experiencing difficulty in finding sufficient liquid capital for development.

During 1970, two Special General Meetings were held to regularise the credit to members' share accounts of filled dividend stamp books and give authority to the Board 'to avail itself of other banking facilities.' Members also approved a proposal that at least £8,000 should be credited to the Education and Member Relations Fund based on a budgeted expenditure presented by the Education and Member Relations Committee not less than one month before the end of the preceding financial year.

The annual accounts for the year ended January 1971 revealed a trading profit of £16,000 with no interim dividend from CWS. The major problem was the unprofitability of non-food departments. Profit from the sale of property was now being transferred to a Property Revenue Fund, which was to be used to help finance developments. The annual report also showed that a pilot scheme to introduce bonus stamps in garages was being extended and 15 petrol stations were issuing stamps in the society's area.

Sales for the year ended January 1972 reached nearly £18 million, and the trading surplus was the highest produced for a 52-week period for over a decade. The Society's mutual trading operation was reorganised into a 52-week credit system with fortnightly collections, and a new Home Shopping Service was introduced. The accounts, which for the first time were produced in columnar form, showed share capital amounting to just over £2 million held by 218,034 members.

Along with other retailers in the UK, the Society experienced rapid expansion in turnover in the first half of the 1970s mainly due to increasing inflation, which also had the effect of increasing overheads, particularly personnel costs. Rising expenses were countered by introducing improved techniques and systems, which at first allowed modest improvements to the Society's reserves. Progress was further hampered in 1974 by the introduction of the three-day week, a bread strike, and a shortage in the supply of sugar; but in spite of these difficulties increased turnover was achieved in the food departments. However, non-food business was less buoyant due to the introduction of Valued Added Tax (VAT).

In the annual report to members for January 1974, the Management Committee reported increased expenses in spite of the cessation of Selective Employment Tax (SET), but a more optimistic note was sounded in reporting a modest increase in share capital for the first time in 18 years. It was also decided at that time to implement the Society's rule requiring members to hold £1 share capital. Those members holding less than one pound ceased to be registered members, their balances being transferred to a share suspense account until they reached the minimum holding, when they were reinstated. In January 1974, the Society had nearly 204,000 members, of whom 124,000 were fully paid.

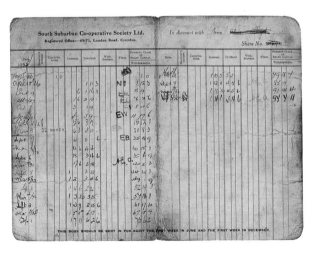

SSCS Members Share Pass Book showing accumulated dividends and interest

Trade Recession

The second half of 1975 saw the commencement of recession in trade, and in its January 1976 report, the Management Committee observed, 'Perhaps the best measure of our progress is the share of the available market in our trading area, and in this sphere we calculate that the Society's share in food increased from 4.5 to 5.6 per cent in two years.' Although sales for the year had increased by 25 per cent, costs had also gone up, resulting in a decrease in surplus on the previous year. Nevertheless, the Committee decided to maintain the dividend stamp bonus to members at double the basic rate of 10p per book redeemed.

In spite of the uncertain national economic situation, the Society improved and modernised 11 food shops and converted 13 others during the five years ended January 1976. In addition, it opened its first freezer centre at Sydenham during 1972, followed two years later by a second unit at Coulsdon. The Redhill store was converted to a superstore in November 1974, four off-licences were opened, an inflatable footwear warehouse was installed at the rear of the Croydon store, and three branches were closed. However, by far the most exciting project was the lease of a 3½ acre site at Beddington Lane, Croydon, for the building of a new food distribution centre. After three years' work, the Centre was opened on schedule and within budget on 20th September 1976. The 100,000 square foot warehouse cost over £2 million, which was financed from profit retained in previous years, without recourse to a loan negotiated with the CWS.

A number of propositions were received from members for consideration at the Society's business meetings, along with recommendations from the Management Committee which required the convening of a Special General Meeting. Members debated suggestions for the foundation of a new society for the south east; the setting up of a special committee to review democratic procedures in the Society; the notification of shop closures to members and staff; and revised election arrangements. By far the most persistent subject debated was the Co-operative Party, its funding and constitution within the Society's rules. It was the subject of two Special General Meetings and a member's proposal. It was clear that, in spite of changes being approved by members, the Management Committee was unable to agree to the request to call a Special General Meeting to change the rule in the terms agreed. At a Special General Meeting held in July 1974, the Management Committee reported that meetings had been held with the Co-operative Party Committee at which it was agreed to incorporate certain aspects of the agreed resolution into a new proposal for consideration by the members. The preamble to the proposal explained there was, 'The need to define more clearly the relationship between the Board and the Co-operative Party Committee to ensure a regulator for future Boards and Committees, and the need to marry the proposed grant to the actual requirement of the Committee.' The recommendation was carried by an overwhelming majority.

These protracted discussions caused a domino effect in relation to the funding of the Education and Member Relations Committee. A proposal was received for consideration at the July 1976 General Meeting to improve the grant to this Committee, and it was approved by a large majority. However, the Board indicated that it wished to appraise the Committee's function before initiating the appropriate rule change, which was approved by the members the following year.

The national recession in trade continued to bite in the second half of the decade, eroding the performance of most retailers. The Society's annual report and accounts for the year ended January 1977 revealed an improvement in published reserves over the previous year. As a pointer to the Society's increasing financial strength, the Board reported that, 'Over the period of ten years since 1967, the published reserves have increased from £399,000 to £4,079,078 including a Tax Equalisation Fund of £978,181. This compares with a decrease of £173,000 in the published reserves for the previous ten years.'

In 1977, the Penny Bank small savings scheme was phased out and replaced by a savings facility based on 10p savings stamps. Longer term savings were encouraged with the launch of Unit Loans at attractive rates of interest. In July of that year, George Warren the Society's Chief Executive took early retirement having completed 47 years' service with the Society. He was replaced by Norman Bingham, who joined the Society from United Drapery Stores.

The final three years to 1980 saw a modest increase in sales although rapidly increasing costs were having an adverse effect on profitability. The pattern of releasing reserves in order to provide the necessary resources to make proposed allocations, which had been evident in earlier years, began to re-establish itself, although liquidity was helped by a large tax refund. In order to encourage members to save, their bonus on completed dividend stamp books was increased to 25p per book in January 1978, making each completed book worth 75p. 1978 also marked the Society's Diamond Jubilee, which was celebrated by promotional events, competitions in major stores, a membership campaign and staff functions. An interesting venture was reported in July 1979 when the Society, with the CWS, decided to launch a Members' Lottery. This was a voluntary scheme for members who wished to stake their 25p bonus on a completed stamp book in the lottery. Instead of the bonus being credited to share accounts, a lottery ticket was received and prizes ranging up to £1,000 were available for winning members. Subsequent reports to members do not record the success or otherwise of the scheme.

A fall in reserves in 1979 prompted discussions with the CWS concerning the Society participating in its regional warehousing scheme, but it was decided not to take part.

In spite of the shortfall in profitability, the Society continued its development strategy and experimented with new ideas. A further 13 shops were modernised or converted, several small dairies purchased and freezer centres opened at Stoneleigh, Bellingham and Oxted. By 1980, the Society was operating 40 off-licences and it had created new traffic offices at Peall Road, replaced a number of vehicles and opened a training centre in Croydon. The building of the new distribution centre had released three acres of land for development at the rear of London Road, Croydon. The CWS Retail and Property Development Services division reviewed the site and studied alternative proposals. This resulted in the doubling of the existing food area, the provision of a new freezer centre and customer refreshment facilities, and the introduction of a travel agency. Whilst purchasing a number of freeholds of existing shops, the Society took the opportunity to close a number of loss-making units. In a further effort to attract trade, the Society launched 'Co-op 600' grocery shops as an experiment in the concept of providing food items at really low prices by concentrating on a minimum of 600 varieties of groceries. The first shop was opened at Sidcup in 1979, followed by Burnt Ash Lane a year later.

Propositions on numerous subjects for the consideration of members continued to be received. These included notification of store closures; changes in the eligibility qualifications for members attending Co-operative Congress and CWS Meetings; the non-stocking of South African goods which had been agreed in 1972 but was rejected in 1978; the provision of creche facilities at members' meetings, with the convening of more meetings during the day; and the re-establishment of recording members' purchases through computer technology.

The continuing saga of the possibility of setting up a South Eastern Co-operative Society by links with the Royal Arsenal or other societies in the region, re-surfaced as a proposition for debate at the Half Yearly Meeting in 1979. The proposed link with Royal Arsenal was rejected by a two to one vote against, whilst an amendment suggesting links with other societies in the vicinity was approved by a similar margin. This decision prompted the distribution of a circular from the Co-operative Union endorsing the initiative, pointing out the scope in the south east for general re-organisation of services, promotional activity and store development opportunities. History again repeated itself and, following discussions on the proposal, Invicta Society decided not to join a larger grouping.

Losses and Rationalisation

The four year period in the run-up to the merger with the CWS in July 1984 was a period of national turndown in business, company liquidations and growing unemployment. It was in 1981 that the Society sold its Regional Distribution Centre (RDC) in Croydon to the CWS along with its Sutton and Orpington operations, in order to provide capital for re-development.

The Society's turnover reached its peak in the year ended January 1981 at £56.2. million, and thereafter fell steadily to £47 million. It suffered trading losses for the three years from 1980 to 1982, and the Management Committee summed up the society's difficulties in its January 1982 report to members in the following words:

> The national recession remained with us throughout 1981 with ever rising costs making trading conditions increasingly difficult particularly when operating from fragmented selling space. A lack of sufficient properly equipped modern shopping facilities remains one of the three major problems facing the Society...

The second was the under-utilisation of the RDC by other societies. The report went on, 'The crippling cost of distribution to the branches from the RDC precludes the Grocery division from contributing a profit. This is critical to the Society's trading result as grocery accounts for over 65 per cent of the Society's trading turnover.' Costs were reduced after September 1981 when the RACS joined the system, following Invicta's entry in the previous September, thereby guaranteeing its future at full capacity.

The third reason contained in the report was that, '(The) non-food division has had heavy trading losses for more than a decade largely as a result of endeavouring to run small departmental stores from premises which have become outdated through changing business and social conditions.'

To address these problems, the Society disposed of uneconomic units, resulting in heavy redundancies. One of the experiments to avoid substantial job losses was the setting up a specialist delicatessen and butchery business under the name of 'Bon Appetit'. Three shops were opened at Chislehurst, West Wickham and Orpington, but the venture was short-lived. Surpluses on the sale of assets and investments together with appropriations from reserves bolstered the weakening financial position. Profitable food shops were re-equipped, whilst non-food stores were redeployed, being converted to Homemaker units. By the end of 1981, 90 per cent of the Society's grocery branches had been re-fixtured.

Discussions with the RACS on the formation of a South East Society were discontinued early in 1982 when, after the completion of a feasibility study by both societies, it was decided that it was in the best interests of all concerned not to proceed.

In 1982, a corporate development plan was produced by management and approved by the Board. The first objective was to phase out a number of non-food units. Sidcup and Tonbridge stores closed in July and August 1982 respectively, along with fuel depots which had experienced a falling off in demand for solid fuels. Further rationalisation followed: 22 grocery shops, six non-food shops, butchery units, the non-food warehouse, a meat factory and warehouse, and a produce centre all closed, and the funds raised were re-invested. In 1983, the Society employed 1200 staff, a reduction of over 300 on the previous year and a fall of over 40 per cent from the position in 1973.

In an effort to recover falling food turnover, the Society purchased the lease of a fully equipped Keymarket store in Penge early in 1983 at a cost of £1.25 million. Trading commenced in February 1983 and, whilst this had the desired effect, the Society was still experiencing problems with supplies from the RDC which impacted adversely on its grocery sales. During the first half of 1983, Norman Bingham resigned as Chief Executive, after six years service, to join the Belfast Society as General Manager. His place was taken by William F Menhenick, the Society's Financial Controller who had been employed by the Society since 1971.

Although merger talks with Royal Arsenal had been discontinued, discussions were taking place with the Invicta Society, and a working party was formed from both societies to consider this proposal. However, Invicta could see no economic reason for joining any of its neighbouring societies at that time, and took the view that it must use its best endeavours to ensure that it moved towards being a thriving and viable society as soon as possible.

In spite of this disappointment, the Society continued to experiment with new trading opportunities. Unprofitable grocery operations were being converted to electrical and video units, 14 centres being opened in the first half of 1983. At this time, a car-hire business was acquired by Covell Properties Ltd, the Society's subsidiary company. Gift and fancy shops, trading as 'Pastels', were opened at Orpington, Tonbridge and West Wickham, and showed early promise and a modest profit. All to no avail.

In its January 1984 annual report, the Management Committee conceded that:

> (The) closing of units in the previous year and subsequent opening of a new superstore have not had the desired effect of reducing the Society's losses. Increased competiton within our trading area coupled with the continuing decline in gross margins, particularly in the grocery business have taken their toll...

At the conclusion of the Annual General Meeting, a Special General Meeting was convened containing a recommendation of the Management Committee that the Society transfer its engagements to the CWS. The recommendation was approved by the requisite two-thirds majority and subsequently confirmed at a further Special General Meeting by a simple majority. The merger became effective in July 1984.

CHAPTER 13
THE EDUCATIONAL SCENE AND POLITICAL ACTIVITY: 1945 to 1985

ROYAL ARSENAL CO-OPERATIVE SOCIETY

Education at Work

How did the Co-op see its future educational role following World War II? John Attfield's *With Light of Knowledge* comments:

> In the educational field, the co-operative movement put forward the demand for the state to recognise the place of the movement within the educational structure, including the provision of grants on the lines of the WEA. Co-operative educationalists planned for a higher level of advanced and specialist training within the movement, with the aim of producing a new generation of co-operative leaders and managers as well as an educated rank and file. This aim was expressed above all in the opening, in 1945, of a greatly expanded Co-operative College, at Stanford Hall near Loughborough.

In 1947, George Durham left the London Society to join the RACS as its Educational Secretary. In the Education Committee's report on Adult Education for 1946/47 satisfaction was expressed that nearly 100 classes had been organised, indicating, 'that a sound basis of class organisation had been achieved.' It also reported that it was 'happy' with the new relationships created with the Surrey and Kent County Education Committees as well as the maintenance of existing courses held in conjunction with the Labour Party. Direct contact was made with Local Education Authorities at the expense of the WEA, and there was a considerable increase in the number of orchestras, choirs and dramatic groups. Lecture courses and lecture film shows were well supported, and as a result there was an increase in the number of tutors and lecturers, with the total reaching 150, of which nearly 100 undertook some form of work.

It was after the war that staff training ceased to be the obligation of the Education Department and became the joint responsibility of a Staff Training Council made up of representatives from the General and Education Committees, the Workers' Advisory Council and Society officials. The full responsibility was taken over by the Society in 1958 and, at that time, George Durham became Staff Training Organiser, his position as Education

Secretary being assumed by Basil Loveridge, who had been the Society's adult education organiser from 1945-47. John Attfield recalls that Loveridge introduced courses on safety in industry, shop steward training and trade union studies and was particularly interested in colonial liberation. In an article in the Society for Co-operative Studies' Journal of January 1998, Loveridge explains that he wanted to prove that education for co-operators – which in his opinion has been sadly neglected – was still a worthwhile policy. To achieve this he proposed a package agreed with the University of London and the WEA, but this was rejected by the Education Committee. In frustration he left in two years, to re-join the United Nations, and was replaced by Rose Garland, the Assistant Education Secretary.

New Horizons

The changing pattern of retailing in the 1950s and the need to exercise tighter financial controls placed additional burden on educational work, which was funded on a fixed percentage, at first stationary, but later falling in real terms, of the Society's surplus. Following discussions with the General Committee, the members of the Society approved in June 1959 a change to a fixed sum of 1s 4d per member per year. To economise, the department moved from Parsons Hill to smaller accommodation at Park Vista, Greenwich, where it stayed until 1977, when it moved back to Powis Street. Activities were curtailed, and the Metropolitan Co-operative Education Committee (formerly the LJEC) ceased to play a prominent role and became limited to a consultancy function. Some indication of the cut-backs can be seen in the reduced numbers of students taking part in RACS classes from 1,750 in 1946/1947 to 1,000 in 1960/1961. The number of cultural groups fell and the annual choral and drama festivals were discontinued in 1958 and 1959. The Peckham film society closed in 1959 followed by Tooting in 1961. Woolwich survived until new societies were formed at Charlton and Slough at the end of the 1960s. In spite of these contractions, new horizons were coming into view.

Well Hall Youth Club

It was in the spring of 1959 that the Education Committee decided that, because of the rapidly changing relationships between the younger and older members in the adolescent age group, they would experiment with the setting up of junior Co-operative Youth Clubs to cover the ages of 14 to 17 years. In 1961, following the Annual Education Conference, it was decided to embrace all young people between 15 and 21 years of age. The first experiments were launched at Falconwood and Coldharbour, Eltham, when 60 young people enrolled on the first evening.

In the same year, another experiment in member relations was held at Catford when nearly 1,000 new members were sent personal invitations to meet the Chairman of the Society and members of the Education Committee to learn of the social and educational facilities provided by the Education Department. Nearly 100, more than half of them under 40 years of age, came along. This successful experiment, later extended to other areas, would not have been possible without the help and guidance of the South Suburban Society.

In June 1961, the Education Committee sponsored a motor cycle club, following a request from the Morden Youth Club, and 77 joined.

The 1960s was a period of rapid expansion in the Society's trading area following mergers with nine societies in Kent, Surrey and Hampshire. Some of these had little or no member education whilst others had a long history and tradition. John Attfield recounts:

> In particular the Sheerness and District Economical Co-operative Society traced its history back as far as 1816, and still played a prominent part in the cultural life of the Isle of Sheppey. The Faversham and Thanet, Addlestone and District, and Slough and District societies each had substantial and active educational organisations. The Gravesend Society had a full-time educational staff and an active policy of auxiliary and youth development including long-standing support for the Co-operative Youth Movement; whilst the Guildford and District Society had a tradition of radical educational policies and had been an early supporter of the Woodcraft Folk.

Thus, the Education Committee had to meet these diverse priorities, merge the various views into their policy and adapt to changing conditions with tighter financial resources.

One of the most exciting things to happen in RACS educational work for a long time was the formation of a class for young mothers at Progress Hall, Eltham, with the provision of a creche for their children whilst they studied.

Education policy in the early 1960s was to help and encourage adult Guilds and the Woodcraft Folk, provide training for potential and existing branch officers, and conduct recruitment campaigns. Adult education was to be furthered by studies in co-operative, social and economic studies; problems of retail distribution; consumer and liberal education; handicrafts and keep fit

Woodcraft Folk with Polish Visitors

classes, whilst the training of youth leaders was considered important in view of the ageing auxiliaries and the generation gap.

Rose Garland resigned toward the end of 1964, after 15 years in the Education Department, to join the Society's Staff Training Department, and her place was taken by Bill May from the St Albans Co-operative Society.

In the autumn of that year, a Young Members' Organisation was formed, sponsored by the Education Committee and later to affiliate to the League of Co-operators. This proved to be a lively organisation which published a straight-talking controversial bulletin containing articles and items of topical interest on trading, democratic and educational affairs.

The mid-point of the decade saw the Education Committee move into the field of education for retirement, to be followed by the publication of a *Co-operative Newsletter* with, 'The idea to meet and fulfil a need by thanking co-operators for views, ideas and opinions concerning contemporary co-operative affairs and for stimulating forward-looking discussions on the many controversial issues facing the Movement.'

In the Society's publication *News of the RACS* at the beginning of 1966, it was stated that society (in its broadest sense) with its rapidly changing standard of values no longer required us (the Co-op), 'To provide formal education... The state now takes care of the three Rs. We must therefore seek out the new needs and desires of our members, and the public at large. Secondly, our endeavours must be where we serve the greatest number of members; thirdly, our programme must be such that the participants, through experience, move closer to the ideals of the co-operation.'

Later in the same year, a Pre-School playgroup was formed at Avery Hill, Eltham, and it was announced that six adult classes with child minder service were being held.

Whilst work within the field of adult education, dealing with social and cultural affairs, was considered to be of great importance, especially with regard to the

Member and Consumer Information

maintenance of democracy, a greater emphasis was being placed on consumer education, 'To guide consumers in choosing well, buying wisely and understanding the legislation which protects them.' This took the form of displays in shops, and at dividend paying stations and Consumer Advisory Evenings held in conjunction with the trading management.

Internationalism was also an issue to which the Education Committee attached great importance. Information was dispensed about the international co-operative movement and life in other countries. Later, the Vietnam war became an important issue – with propositions appearing on agendas of members' meetings. The Education Department frequently received delegations and visitors from overseas, and participated in study hours and reciprocal events abroad.

The first year of the decade saw the death in March of Joe Reeves (the Committee's influential Secretary during the inter-war years), an increase in the education grant – now in the new decimal currency – and the reorganisation of the work of the Education Department into Eastern and Western areas with an office in Woking.

Greater Democracy

Member involvement had been an important issue throughout the Movement in the 1960s. The 1960 Blackpool Congress decided to call on societies to encourage 'a deeper sense of responsibility among members in the well-being of their societies.' The challenge of promoting business efficiency in the climate of fierce competition and decreasing margins, and calls for improving member participation, threw into sharp contrast the needs of professional management to run the business and their frustration with interference from lay members. Within the RACS, a Rules Revision Committee in 1961/62 advocated, amongst other things, the introduction of half-yearly instead of quarterly meetings, the restriction of debate on matters relating to Society business and an extension of the powers of the full-time General Committee. An unofficial 'Keep the RACS Democratic Committee' was formed to oppose the majority report. Support came from all sections of the membership and auxiliary organisations, and over 1,500 members attended the Special General Meetings when the majority of the recommendations were rejected. The 'Keep the RACS Democratic Committee' set up a new unofficial pressure group called 'Co-operative Advance' and, for a number of years, campaigned for greater democracy in the RACS.

Perhaps the greatest controversy between the Education Committee and the Society was the introduction of dividend stamps in place of the traditional cash dividend in 1967. Some saw the stamps as a trading promotional tool, whilst others looked upon them as a retreat from co-operative principles. In March 1970, the General Committee recommended their adoption, and this was opposed by the Education Committee, its auxiliaries, and the Political Purposes Committee. A total of 2,600 members attended the meetings, and the proposal failed by 400 votes to achieve the necessary two-thirds majority. The General Committee called further meetings two months later when the proposal was approved by 2,401 in favour and 661 against.

The Education Committee continued to be busy organising special conferences, projects and discussion groups on matters of topical interest throughout its Kent, London and Western districts. Whilst membership of the adult auxiliaries was falling, the Woodcraft Folk continued to flourish, with 55 groups operating by 1975. The Committees work on the international scene, which included participation in overseas study visits, entertaining foreign visitors and receiving overseas students from the Co-operative College on an annual basis, was marked by it being listed by the Council of Europe as being among the organisations involved in education for international understanding.

Overseas Visitors to RACS from the Co-operative College
(Arnold Bonner, tutor, in centre)

The mid-point of the decade saw the Committee lobbying Parliament to express its concern with the Government's cutbacks in education, which had resulted in the restriction of nursery education, the closure of youth centres, and deteriorating school conditions. In the following year, the department's offices moved from Park Vista, Greenwich, to Powis Street, Woolwich, and it was from this base in 1977 that the centenary of education work in the Society was launched. To mark the occasion, a conference was held at the Hotel New Ambassadors, in central London, with the theme 'Co-operative Education in the 1980s' and, later in the year, a concert of song, dance and wine was held in Greenwich Borough Hall.

In September 1978, Bill May left the Society after 14 years' service to take up an appointment with the Co-operative Union, and was succeeded by Roy Martin, the Assistant Secretary. In the following year the London and Western Joint Co-operative Councils were formed, following the successful pilot scheme in Kent, and the decade ended with the Committee supporting the ICA's 'Buy a Bucket of Water' appeal as part of the United Nation's International Year of the Child.

It was in 1981 that the Education Committee met with the General Committee to discuss dividend policy. They also agreed to the freezing of their grant in view of the deteriorating financial position of the Society. Area Members' Council members raised pertinent questions with the General Committee concerning property disposals and the rationalisation that was taking place in the Society's trading activities.

The first annual Members' Council Congress was held at Lewisham in May 1981, and it was later in that year that John Attfield published his *With Light of Knowledge – A Hundred Years of Education in the RACS.*

The number of members taking part in activities organised by the Education Committee continued to hold steady at just over 5,000. But this masked the continuing decline in the Co-operative Women's Guild and in attendances at local classes, although participation in Area Members' Councils, the Woodcraft Folk and Young Adult Group continued to increase.

International visits, established many years before, were still considered to be an important part of the Committee's cultural programme and, during the period, visits were made to Germany, Italy and China.

Joint educational ventures were encouraged with local societies. Various events were arranged in conjunction with the Invicta Society, whilst support was given to the inauguration of a Young Adult Group in Enfield.

Wider society and co-operative issues were supported when members took part on the People's March for Jobs and various meetings on nuclear disarmament.

When the merger with the CWS took place in 1985, assurances were received that the level of activity being undertaken at that time would continue, along with the provision of services for auxiliaries, organisations and employees. This promise was kept, with the Member Relations staff (the new name was adopted just prior to the merger) becoming part of the management team and responsible to the Branch Secretary.

Political Activity

The post-war work of the Political Purposes Committee was rigidly defined by the rules and standing orders of the parent society. However, within these limitations, a great deal of activity was generated and carried on. After the war finished, much new work had to be developed and new contacts made, and this largely fell on the shoulders of Edwin Furness, who was appointed Secretary in 1946, following Walter H Green, the first full-time Secretary of the Committee, who was to become MP for Deptford.

Political Purposes Committee, 1946

Both before and after the General Election in 1945, the Education and Political Purposes Committees worked closely in securing a Labour victory. *Comradeship* contained numerous articles describing the Party's work. In the RACS trading area Labour made a clean sweep. The area supplied six ministers in the Labour Government and, at the municipal elections in November 1945, nearly all of the 130 candidates on the RACS Local Government Panel were successful, eight of them being elected mayors of their boroughs.

Just after the war, rather poor relations existed with the Co-operative Party, although the Society had affiliated on a token basis for many years. After a short while, an understanding was reached with the National Committee of the Party for the Political Purposes Committee to be fully recognised as a Society Co-operative Party, providing facilities for members to join the Party. This resulted in the end of the small Voluntary Co-operative Party that had been recently established. From then onwards, relationships with the Party and its officials remained cordial.

An interesting arrangement that had been agreed in the early days of the Southern Regional Council of the Labour Party, was for the office of Chairman to rotate in turn between the trade union, the Constituency Labour Party, and the co-operative members of the Regional Council Executive Committee. This resulted in Edwin Furness becoming the first Co-operative Chairman of the Regional Council.

The 1950s saw the Political Purposes Committee following its standard packages of activities – appointing delegates to Co-operative Party and Labour Party conferences, selecting representatives to General Management Committees of the Labour Party, and organising conferences and weekend schools. In 1953, the Committee, in conjunction with the London, Enfield and Watford Co-operative Societies, formed the Labour Party Co-operative Group, which was affiliated to the London Labour Party, and one of the first actions was to place a motion on its agenda concerning the allocation of shop sites to the Movement.

In 1957, difficulties arose in the course of the election of the Committee, when the Returning Officer received complaints concerning solicitation of votes for four highly respected candidates by printed material, contrary to rule, but without their knowledge. The Returning Officer had no alternative but to refer the matter to the Society's Arbitrators, who decided that an infringement had arisen, and this view was upheld, with some reluctance, by the Registrar of Friendly Societies. However, the disqualified candidates were not satisfied with these decisions and took the matter to the High Court where it was held that the material did not amount to solicitation – thus they were re-instated to the Committee.

The 1960s opened with the Labour Party considering its aims and objectives in the light of UK and world conditions. 1962 was the Festival of Labour Year, and its central feature was highlighted in the London arrangements at Battersea Park during two days in June. The Political Purposes Committee spent some time reviewing the Labour Party's home policy, described in a pamphlet under the title *Signposts for the Sixties*, in the hope that members would obtain and read the publication.

The election results for the Greater London Council in 1964 exceeded the expectations of the Labour Party. Much greater interest was shown than was usual – probably because of good press, broadcasting and television coverage. Two members of the Political Purposes Committee were elected, along with the Political Secretary and a member of the Society's Local Government Panel. Three years later, the position was reversed as a result of national rather than local issues.

The Committee joined with the General Committee in an attack on the operation of the Selective Employment Tax. Motions to the Labour Party Conference and the lobbying of Parliament received widespread publicity and may well have added to the growing awareness of the injustices and anomalies inherent in the tax. Protests were also made to the Prime Minister and Minister of Power concerning increases to electricity charges.

In 1968 Co-operative Congress set up a working party to consider the role and effectiveness of the Co-operative Party, with the result that it re-affirmed that Co-operative influence in politics could best be strengthened by the closest possible relationship with the Labour Movement. In its evidence to the working party, the Political Purposes Committee called for the affiliation of the Co-operative Party to the Labour Party in order to strengthen Co-operative influence on Labour policies.

The same year saw the winding up of the London Labour Party after 54 years, and responsibility for co-ordinating Labour Party activity throughout Greater London went to the Greater London Regional Council. The Co-operative Movement had a powerful voice in its affairs through the direct affiliation of the Royal Arsenal and London Societies. The Society had two members elected to the Co-operative section of the Regional Executive.

The considerable extension of the Society's area during the 1960s caused the Political Purposes Committee to consider its relations with local Co-operative Party branches at Woking, Gravesend, Slough and Addlestone. In view of the uncertainty in 1968 about the future form of organisation of the Co-operative Party, the Committee agreed temporary arrangements guaranteeing the existence of the four branches and involved them in the selection of RACS resolutions and delegates for the 1969 Co-operative Party Conference.

The 1970s saw the Committee responding to a resolution of a members' meeting by organising a very successful lobby of Parliament on food prices which was attended by RACS members from South London, Kent and Surrey.

Joint conferences with the Committee's counterparts in the South Suburban and London Societies were arranged on health services and co-operative housing as well as a campaign for the setting up of a Co-operative Development Agency.

From 1931 to 1975 and 1976 to 1978, the Political Committee was successful in securing representation on the National Executive of the Labour Party as the representative for co-operatives, socialist and professional societies. John Cartwright held positions as the Society's Political Secretary, member of the RACS full-time General Committee, and latterly as MP for the Woolwich East Constituency. He was succeeded as Political Secretary in 1972 by Richard Balfe, who was to become a member of the first part-time General Committee of the RACS in 1978, and, in the following year, a Member of the European Parliament (MEP) for London South Inner, a position he still holds.

Lobby of Parliament, 1973

Left to Right:

S. H. Kennard (Gen.Com.); J. Wellbeloved (MP Erith);

B. Hammill (Chair Pol. Com.); H. Lamborn (Gen.Com.) MP Southwark;

C. C. Job (Gen.Com.); R. A. Balfe (Sec. Pol. Com.); Hilda Smith (Pol. Com.);

J. C. Cartwright (Gen.Com.) MP Woolwich; G. F. Hunn (Gen.Com.)

The 1980s saw the Committee endeavouring to stimulate political activity throughout the Society's area, this to be achieved by the appointment of a Political Organiser to work under the Political Secretary. Paul Rossi was recruited following Richard Balfe's success in the European Parliament elections, but after a short while he was succeeded by Glenys Thornton (made a Life Peer in 1998) who held the post up to and following the merger with the CWS.

During the 1980s, the Committee actively participated in the Nuclear Disarmament Campaign; the 600th anniversary celebrations, organised by the Labour Movement, of the Peasants' Revolt on Blackheath; the People's March for Jobs; the campaign to save the GLC and ILEA; and the lobby of Parliament against the abolition of London Transport. It also assisted in sponsoring meetings, arranging discounts, and providing assistance in the Miners' Strike of 1984.

Similar assurances were received from the CWS following the merger concerning the continuation of existing political activity along with the maintenance, in real terms, of affiliation fees payable to Constituency Labour Parties. As with Member Relations staff, the Political Secretary became part of the management team, responsible to the Branch Secretary.

Educational Work

In 1945, conditions were not sufficiently settled for there to be any considerable expansion of educational developments. The war years had seen the death of Elizabeth E M Allen at the age of 74 after 50 years' service to the Movement. She joined the Reigate Society in 1891, and served on its Management Committee for over 20 years, acting for some time as its President. A member of the CWG, she was elected to the Education Committee of the Croydon Society in 1907 and served on the South Suburban Education Committee from 1919 to 1941.

A Staff Training Council, consisting of members of the Management and Education Committees was formed early in 1946, and activity increased in all sections of youth work and adult education during the following two years. William Stewart, the Society's Education Secretary, retired with ill-health in 1947, and two years later a new education development plan was introduced along with the publication of the first education gazette.

A decline in music, social studies and handicraft classes was reported by the Education Committee in 1950, following the imposition of limits on facilities provided by local authorities. To overcome this, a publicity campaign outlining details of the educational facilities available, was directed towards new and existing members, with the result that nearly 600 replies were received. Two years later, two scholarships were established tenable at the Co-operative College, the funding being met jointly by the Management and Education Committees.

The mid-fifties saw the appointment of Henry Pichowski as Education Secretary; numbers of youth group leaders and members declined, and the difficulty in recruiting suitably experienced and qualified leaders did not help to arrest the position. Whilst film shows for adults and children were attracting good audiences, the decline in the Society's fortunes did not allow any financial improvement for educational work, one of the results of which was the relinquishing of 60 Croydon Road, Penge, to reduce adminstrative expenses, making greater use of number 62 for classes, meetings and staff training. The grant from the Society for educational work continued to fall, and it was decided in 1960 to set up a special committee to examine member relations in the Society with the objective of 'finding ways and means of reducing member apathy, raising the morale of members and staff, and increasing member interest in the Society both as a trading and co-operative organisation.'

Educational activities in the decade leading to the early 1970s saw the Education Committee renamed the Education and Member Relations Committee in November 1962. As part of an economy drive, its officials were transferred to Croydon. The Committee continued to support its traditional activities and, in addition, arranged new member events,

CWS publicity film shows and consumer demonstration evenings as well as lecture courses and youth activity. Very successful new members' introductory events commenced in 1966 in spite of declining financial support from the Society and increasing costs. In the same year, a new experiment, jointly financed by the Society and the CWS, a 'Meet Your Food Trades Department Manager' evening, was held at the Fairfield Halls, Croydon. Financial difficulties continued, and, to help relieve the position, the Co-operative Womens Guild agreed to take a 50 per cent reduction in assistance towards hall rents. The situation was helped towards the end of the decade when the education grant was increased to £6,300. In 1969, the Committee held meetings with the Board and Co-operative Party to discuss declining attendance at members' meetings, and it was at this time that Consumer Information Stands were introduced into six stores along with the setting up of a working party for auxiliary development. However, this was shortlived and was discontinued two years later.

In order to improve finances, members of the Society approved a proposal at a Special General Meeting held in 1971 that not less than £8,000 be granted each year to the Education and Member Relations Committee based upon budgeted expenditure produced by it to the Board. This resulted in the setting up, with encouraging results, of Member Education Councils to promote member activity at local level. Special lectures and essay and art competitions for children in secondary schools in the Society's area were arranged by a specially formed Robert Owen Centenary Committee.

The decade from 1970 saw the continuation of the Committee's traditional activities. Branches of the Co-operative Women's Guild continued to meet, but in declining numbers. The Society's young members in the Co-operative Youth Movement (CYM) were active in national events, taking part in the annual conference and public speaking contests. The Woodcraft Folk continued to receive visitors and make visits overseas. The Elizabeth Allen Essay competition continued to attract a reasonable number of entries; the Annual Arts Festival was well supported; horticultural societies held annual shows; and International Co-operative Day celebrations took the form for many years of a concert at the Fairfield Halls, Croydon, and an outdoor event at the South Norwood Recreation Ground.

In addition to these regular activities, the Committee undertook a number of experimental projects designed to improve member participation. In the early 1970s, staff/member weekends were held at Beatrice Webb House, Dorking, to simulate the work of the Management and Education Committees and District Members Councils, but these were discontinued after a short while due to lack of staff support. An experimental membership campaign was held two years later, but it failed to achieve any significant results.

However, consumer open evenings at five stores continued to be popular, with programmes embracing films, product information and sample distribution. These events provided opportunities to carry out consumer surveys for trading and educational purposes. Another innovation was the introduction of 'Meet The Candidate' meetings, when members aspiring to office in the Society met members of co-operative organisations and enunciated their views and thoughts on Society policy and activities.

In 1974, a members' guide to educational groups and services was produced. A Joint Sub-Committee – with the Management Committee – was set up to consider ways and means of improving member participation at elections and members' meetings, but nothing positive came from the discussions.

The rampant inflation of the 1970s drastically affected the Committee's ability to continue to finance its existing activities quite apart from expanding them. The Management Committee failed to approve the Committee's budget, restricting the grant to £12,000. However, in 1977, as a result of pressure from active members, the Board improved the Committee's grant to a more realistic amount.

In the late 1970s, the Committee decided to sponsor several outside activity groups. In 1977, the Croydon Band was renamed the Croydon Co-op Band and regularly performed at Co-operative Day functions and other concerts. This sponsorship continued until the late 1990s. In the Society's Diamond Jubilee Year, the Croydon Judo Club was sponsored and renamed the Croydon Co-operative Budo Centre, and this was followed in the same year by the sponsorship of the Croydon Male Voice Choir. (See Appendix 7)

It was in 1978 that the Committee published a news sheet *Caring and Sharing* which was produced three times a year with the objective of

Croydon Co-op Band at the Fairfield Halls, Croydon

improving communications and stimulating interest in members' activities. The publication was available in the Society's largest shops as well as being posted to member groups.

At the end of the decade, nine branches of the Co-operative Women's Guild were meeting and, whilst the activities of the Woodcraft Folk were expanding, the Co-operative Youth Movement was disbanded. Increasing interest was being shown by grass roots members in the establishment of Co-operative Community Councils (CCC), of which six were operating,

Beckenham Mother and Toddler Group, 1980

some with the assistance of the RACS. At this time, the Employees' Sports Club at Beckenham was becoming a co-operative community centre for co-op groups, young and old. By 1983, six groups were meeting there, including a Pre-School Play Group, a Young Wives Group, a Mothers and Toddlers Group established in the spring of 1980, and a very successful Ladies Keep Fit Group.

When the merger came about in 1984, the Committee was servicing more than 50 in-store Consumer Information dispensers. Six branches of the Co-operative Women's Guild were meeting at Addiscombe, Brixton, Coney Hall, Petts Wood, Thornton Heath, and Wallington. The Horticultural Society organised flower shows at Coulsdon, Beckenham and Tonbridge. Staff induction courses were being held regularly; the Woodcraft Folk

participated in the International Folk Camp held in the grounds of the Co-operative College; and the usual arrangements were made to celebrate International Co-operative Day with a concert in Fairfield Halls, Croydon, and an outdoor fete at South Norwood Recreation Ground. The Society's grant for educational activities at the merger was £34,600.

Beckenham Ladies Keep Fit Group, 1981

137

Political Activities

On the political scene, the Co-operative Party was operating seven local parties, the branches at Reigate and Penge being re-established after the war, with a new branch being set up at Sidcup in 1948. At that time, there were over 380 individual members of the Party, and in two years this had risen to over 460.

Co-operative Party individual membership and local parties remained steady during the decade, and work proceeded along familiar lines – organisation of weekend schools and area conferences. The growth in unemployment created fertile ground for the promotion of Co-operative candidates in local authority elections. This was considered to be one of the most important facets of the Party's work. A new agreement with the Labour Party came into operation in 1959, but no change was made in any of the agreements between the local parties and their respective Labour Parties. A general election was held in the same year, and this dominated the Committee's work, but the Conservatives were returned with an increased majority.

The nature of political activity did not change in the 10 or so years to the early 1970s. It continued to centre on the traditional areas of maintaining links with the Labour Party, through affiliations to Constituency Labour Parties and the Southern and Greater London Regional Councils; supporting candidates in local government elections; operating local parties in the Society's area; and organising conferences, weekend and summer schools.

The Party continued to take an active role in the Labour Party Conference and the Trade Union Congress, making its views known on the various issues of the day, e.g. renouncing nuclear weapons, supporting the Botswana Project, welcoming the withdrawal of troops from the Middle East, supporting the abolition of South African goods from co-op shops, condemning US involvement in Vietnam and the failure to bring the Rhodesian situation to a satisfactory conclusion. Closer to home, it joined in the national protests at the imposition of Selective Employment Tax.

The 1968 Co-operative Congress set up a working party to look into the role and effectiveness of the Co-operative Party and the Society Co-operative Party Committee submitted a memorandum for its consideration. However, no major changes in the Party were forthcoming.

Financial Constraint

As with the parent Society and the Education and Member Relations Committee, the finances of the Society Party were under considerable strain. The basis of the financial grant from the Society had not been changed since 1957. In 1969, the Party had to increase the individual member's annual subscription to five shillings (25p). Following the decision of the members' in 1971 to increase the grant to the Education and Member Relations Committee, and the Society's improved financial performance, the Party

Committee requested the Management Committee to review its grant, but it could not help. Following this rejection, the Management Committee was asked to recommend a change to rule to improve the grant, but it was not prepared to do so. The Party Committee were approached by the National Association of Co-operative Officials (NACO) to implement the salary award to the Political Secretary but it declined, and suggested that NACO approach the Management Committee on its behalf.

The deteriorating financial position of the Society during the 1970s, brought about by rapidly escalating inflation, had a knock-on effect on the ability of the Party Committee to adequately broadcast its message. One of its major economies was the loss in 1973 of Don Storer, its full-time Secretary for 15 years. The Party requested the Management Committee to fund a part-time Secretary but, when the necessary rule-change was put to the members, it was rejected.

At that time, the main focus for political action and discussion by the organising of regular meeting and conferences was provided by the Croydon, Lambeth and Orpington branches of the Party. New branches were formed at East Surrey in 1975 and Bromley Borough the following year.

In its report to members for 1971, the Party Committee highlighted falling living standards and was very critical of the Government's voting alliance with the Liberal Party, increasing unemployment and the minimal advance in the establishment of a Co-operative Development Agency (CDA). Criticism was also levelled against the Government's use of North Sea oil revenue and the operation of Common Market regulations.

In the Society's Diamond Jubilee year, the Party celebrated this landmark with a reception for Party members and representatives from the Society and the Labour Party. At that time, there were 318 members. Criticism was still being made of the Government's failure to adequately fund the CDA or provide technical assistance for new co-operatives. However, it was acknowledged that its establishment was a step forward, with further representation required for it to be provided with proper resources. It was reported that a new branch had been formed that year at Reigate and membership had increased to 331, but by 1980 this had fallen to 274.

Throughout this whole period, the Party continued to support local parties, send delegates to Constituency Labour Parties and play a full part in local political activities. Sponsorship was given to candidates in County Council and GLC elections as well as sponsored nominees in Parliamentary elections. Committee and Party members served on a wide range of public bodies including magistrates, school and hospital governors, consultative councils, community and area health councils and community relations councils.

The Society's published reports for the years ended January 1980 and 1982 did not contain reports of Party activities, and it is presumed that these were submitted as a separate document to members attending these Annual

General Meetings. This procedure was certainly followed at the July, 1982 half yearly meeting, when the report was rejected by members. This action clearly indicated dissatisfaction with the local Party, a situation that was evidenced by a member's proposition submitted to the January 1983 Annual General Meeting that the Society disassociate itself from the local Party and only support the Central Party. The proposal was defeated by 121 votes in favour and 169 against.

The final report to members before the 1984 merger with the CWS reviewed its activities in the General and European elections, its policy decisions and political actions at the Annual Party Conference, and mattters of national and local interest. The Committee also continued with its affiliations and donations.

At the merger, seven branches of the Party at Croydon, Lewisham, Bromley, Lambeth, Sutton, East Surrey and Sevenoaks continued to be active.

CHAPTER 14
CWS: THE COMMERCIAL INHERITANCE

Background

The preceding chapters have charted the birth and decline of two great retail co-operative societies in South London. South Suburban came into being in 1918 as a result of the amalgamation of the Croydon Society (1887), the Bromley and Crays Society (1882), and the Penge and Beckenham Society (1879). They were joined later by the Reigate and Tonbridge Societies and, by the outbreak of the Second World War, the South Suburban Society was the fourth largest retail society in the country.

After a number of years of trading difficulties, the Society merged with the CWS in July 1984. At that time, the Society had been incurring losses (before surplus on the sale of assets) at the rate of £3.7 million per annum. Annual trade amounted to £47 million, and there were 1,380 employees.

The Society's non-food business of £2 million was conducted through 13 shops with 180 employees. Food sales totalling £28 million were achieved through 48 shops and one superstore, which were staffed by 725 employees. The dairy department employed 310 staff and had an annual trade of £9 million. It was profitable but its premises and equipment were in poor condition. Employees engaged in services and administration totalled 165, most of these being based at the Society's Croydon headquarters.

The Royal Arsenal Co-operative Society was established in Woolwich by engineers employed in the Royal Ordnance factory in 1868. It became one of the country's largest and strongest societies, merging in the 1960s with nine neighbouring societies and, by 1970, total sales had reached £43 million. During the next few years, the Society started to lose ground and, in spite of various rationalisation plans and independent advice, could not stem its trading loses. The Society merged with the CWS in February 1985 and, although its asset base was still quite strong, it had been incurring losses at the rate of £5.9 million per annum. Annual trade amounted to £150 millions, and there were 3,670 employees.

The non-food trade of £6.9 million per annum was conducted through seven department stores employing 240 staff. The food business of £56 million per annum was carried on though 72 units employing 1,370 staff. The Society operated four superstores with annual sales of £33.5 million and employing 760 people. Administration and services, based at Woolwich, employed 199 staff.

The RACS also had significant and largely profitable trade in other divisions. In the milk business, the RACS had closed its Mitcham processing dairy in April 1984, as part of a regional processing rationalisation plan undertaken by the CWS, Kent Society, South Suburban Society and Royal Arsenal Society. At the merger in February 1985, the RACS milk distribution business was transferred to this group. At that time, this business was worth £25.6 million, including sales from Co-operative Dairy Society, a separate subsidiary society operating from Guildford.

The RACS had been operating travel bureaux since the 1930s which, at that time, were part of a much larger coach and transport operation. The coach operation closed in 1982, but the travel business expanded with the increase in package holidays and tours. At the time of the merger, the Society had 20 travel bureaux with a turnover of £10 million and a long record of profitable trading.

There is little doubt that the reputation of the RACS Funeral Service was second to none in South East London. Following the merger with the CWS, the 21 funeral offices of the RACS were incorporated into the South East Region of the CWS, bringing the total number of outlets to 34 with 160 staff.

In addition to these trading operations the RACS held a wide portfolio of non-trading properties. Amongst these was a sports ground in the Footscray Road, New Eltham, purchased from the Furness Withey shipping line in 1947. Three years later, F. J. Comerton, Chairman of the General Committee unveiled a plaque on new entrance gates erected as a memorial to employees who died in the two World Wars. For many years 'the ground', as it was known by its regular visitors, was a popular venue for employees and their families, but due to escalating costs was closed in 1999.

Integration

During 1984 and 1985, the specialist trading and financial resources of the CWS were linked to the corresponding departments of the South Suburban and Royal Arsenal Societies. The South Suburban Leslie Park dairy became part of the Kent Co-operative Society, and the milk rounds of both Societies joined the CWS milk group. Similarly, funeral, travel and fuel services joined the CWS groups in those businesses, whilst the chemist shops were transferred to the National Co-operative Chemists.

Food and non-food retailing, services and administration were formed into a group which became part of the CWS Retail Division, with John Owen appointed as Group General Manager, and Ron Roffey as Branch Secretary (to be re-designated later as Regional Adminstrator). The management and administration of both Societies were integrated, and from June 1985 were based at Woolwich. The South East Retail Group was born.

The Management Committees of both Societies became Branch Committees of the CWS and met at monthly intervals with the Group General Manager and Branch Secretary in attendance. The Committees received reports on trading and other activities and, from time to time, met senior managers of other CWS groups, as well as meeting together at regular intervals. Initially, the CWS Board appointed Mr T A Deacon and Mr R G Bennett, two of its members, to take a particular interest in South East operations. Both CWS Directors and Management met with the Branch Committees and visited units from time to time.

For the 1985 financial year ending on 11th January 1986, sales included in CWS accounts derived from 48 weeks' trading in the Royal Arsenal Branch and a full year in the South Suburban Branch, and totalled £160 million. Losses amounted to £1.1 million and interest charges arising from the transfers were about £3.6 million. CWS reserves were increased by £7.5 million as a result of the transfers.

Capital investment in the region reached £3 million in 1985, whilst the sale of various assets during the year yielded £8 million.

The total number of employees in the first 18 months following the merger fell by 695 to 3,850, of whom 2,900 were employed in the retail group, the remainder being in the milk, funerals and travel businesses. Whilst some job losses occurred through natural wastage, most were by redundancies.

The thoughtful and considerate attitude of the trade unions and their members, together with the active and helpful participation of the Co-operative Union, were significant factors in ensuring that the mergers were brought to a successful conclusion, and that a viable co-operative business was maintained in the south east.

As the Co-operative Union Report to Congress, 1985, stated:

> The area of major concern, however, was the Metropolitan Region, and the transfer of the South Suburban Society to the CWS, followed early in 1985 by the transfer of the Royal Arsenal Society to the CWS, received the whole-hearted support of the Co-operative Union. The problems of the Metropolitan Societies have been of major and growing concern to the Movement nationally and this opportunity to resolve them represents the most important development in the area of regionalisation for many years.

These successful mergers significantly increased the CWS's retail business and provided a platform for it to promote further mergers with independent retail societies in the North West, East Midlands, North London and the South East. This latter series of mergers, with Sittingbourne (September 1988), Invicta (November 1993), and Brighton (October 1994), are of particular interest as they became part of Co-op South East, the name by which the South East Retail Group was to become known. These mergers coupled with the Society's sale of its manufacturing interests changed the core business of the CWS from manufacturing to retailing.

APPENDIX 1
ROYAL ARSENAL CO-OPERATIVE SOCIETY FOUNDER AND GENERAL COMMITTEE MEMBERS 1868 to 1985

NAME	TITLE	BORN	DIED	SERVICE
Adams, G D	Mr	*	*	Pre 1896. Chair
Allard, C	Mr	*	*	Pre 1896
Alsford, J	Mr	*	*	1868. Founder
Ambler, R	Mr	*	*	Pre 1896
Anderson, F	Mr	*	*	Pre 1896
Arnold, John	Mr	1837	12 July 1905	Pre 1896
Arnold, Jos	Mr	*	*	Pre 1896
Ashworth, W	Mr	*	*	In period 1896 - 1920 Chair
Baker, G	Mr	*	*	Pre 1896
Baker, P	Mr	*	*	Pre 1896
Bale, E J	Mr	1902	*	1927 - 1934
Balfe, R A	Mr, BSc, GLC, MEP	14 May 1944	*	1978 - 1984
Bamforth, R	Mr	*	*	Pre 1896
Baxendale, E	Mr	1841	*	Pre 1896
Bennett, G N	Mr, FCIS, JP, MBIM, FCCA	19 Dec 1915	29 Sept 1979	1952 - 1978 Chair

Bevan, G	Mr	*	June, 1909	1868. Founder
Bilney, P H	Mr	28 June 1893	8 May 1962	1948 - 1958
Blagden, W	Mr	*	*	1868. Founder
Blaseby, C A	Mr	28 Nov 1903	27 Mar 1986	1937 - 1945; 1958 - 1968. Chair
Bool, G R	Mr, JP	27 May 1934	*	1984 - 1985
Bowra, A J	Mr	18 Oct 1925	*	1984 - 1985
Brownlie, J T	Mr, CBE	1865	1938	1903 - 1909
Bull, E J	Mr	*	*	Pre 1920
Burgess, J	Mrs, Mayor, JP	24 Mar 1891	6 Jan 1981	1946 - 1948
Byford, C	Mr	1851	25 July 1901	Pre 1896
Byford, R	Mr	16 Jan 1849	*	Pre 1896
Callaghan, E A	Mrs	*	*	In period 1896 - 1920
Callaghan, H E	Mr	5 July 1894	May 1965	1946 - 1948
Cartwright, J C	Mr, MP, JP	29 Nov 1933	*	1972 - 1974
Cash, A	Mr	*	*	Pre 1920
Chambers, F	Mr	*	*	Pre 1920. Chair
Chambers, T	Mr	*	*	Pre 1896. Chair
Chasteauneuf, E	Mr	*	*	Pre 1896
Coleman, J C	Mr	15 Sept 1901	1970	1947 - 1962. Chair
Coles, T	Mr	*	*	1868. Founder
Comerton, F J	Mr, JP	22 June 1893	30 Dec 1969	1927 - 1954; 1956 - 1958. Chair
Conolly, W	Mr	*	*	1868. Founder

Corina, J	Mr	18 Feb 1910	27 May 1982	1935 - 1957. Chair
Coventry, S	Mr	*	*	1868. Founder
Curtis, S	Mr	1862	*	1923
Dashwood, A T	Mr, JP	*	*	1896 - 1903. Chair; 1933 - 1935
Davis, J	Mr	*	*	Pre 1896
Davis, W T	Mr	6 Jul 1872	*	From 1913. Chair
Day, S M	Mrs	13 Jan 1927	*	1974 - 1982
Deans, A	Mr	*	*	Pre 1896. Chair
Dennett, A	Mr, CSD	18 Oct 1906	30 Oct 1978	1946 - 1951
Dickinson, J	Mr	1870	12 Mar 1944	1908 - 1917. Chair
Ditton, H	Mr	18 Oct 1898	2 Jul 1961	1948 - 1952
Dixon, K	Mr	7 Oct 1940	1990	1984 - 1985
Dowd, M	Mr	*	*	Pre 1896
Easton, J	Mr	*	*	Pre 1896
Elder, R	Mr	*	*	Pre 1896
Elliott, G	Mr	*	*	Pre 1896
Ellis, E	Mr	*	*	Pre 1896
Ellis, H C	Mr	16 Dec 1898	1960	1935 - 1946
Enticknap, D T	Mr	16 Nov 1930		1984 - 1985
Fairley, J	Mr	*	*	1868. Founder
Farrell, J	Mr	1862	3 July 1926	1904 - 1916; 1920. Chair
Farrell, W N	Mr, BEM	26 Jun 1918		1978 - 1984

Feakes, T	Mr	*	*	Pre 1896
Fitzpatrick, T	Mr	*	*	Pre 1896
Forst, G	Mr	*	*	In period 1896 - 1920
Fort, G	Mr	*	*	Pre 1896
Foster, G	Mr	*	3 Dec 1908	1881 - 1909. Chair
Foster, N	Mr	*	*	In period 1896 - 1920
Frost, G	Mr	*	*	Pre 1896
Frost, R	Mr	*	*	Pre 1896
Gillender, J	Mr	*	*	Pre 1896
Gould, J	Mr	*	*	Pre 1896
Grant, G	Mr	*	*	Pre 1896
Gray, D	Mr	*	*	Pre 1896
Green, E	Mr	*	*	Pre 1896
Green, J	Mr	*	*	Pre 1896. Chair
Grey, D	Mr	*	*	*
Hainsworth, A	Mr	7 Nov 1863	22 Aug 1922	In period 1896 - 1920
Hall, G	Mr	*	*	In period 1896 - 1920
Halsey, N L	Mr	16 Jan 1919		1974 - 1984
Hamblin, G	Mr	*	*	In period 1896 - 1920
Hammond, J	Mr	*	*	Pre 1896
Handley, I L	Mrs	21 Jan 1924		1979 - 1984
Harris, J	Mr	May 1860	23 Feb 1916	From c1890
Harwood, S	Mr	*	*	Pre 1896

Heard, T	Mr	1844	8 July 1901	From 1880. Chair
Henderson, G J	Mr	29 Oct 1851	Oct 1915	Pre 1915
Henning, L M	Mrs, FSCT Cert Ed	29 Oct 1923		1982 - 1985
Henrotte, E	Mrs	28 Jun 1896	27 Sept 1981	1939 - 1959
Hickling, J	Mr	*	*	Pre 1896
Hill, C	Mr	*	*	Pre 1896
Hoare, W	Mr	*	*	1868. Founder
Hollidge, C	Mr	*	*	Pre 1896
Hunn, G F	Mr	15 Feb 1929		1962 - 1964; 1968 - 1985 Chair
Illidge, J	Mr	*	*	In period 1896 - 1920
Jeff, J	Mr	*	*	Pre 1896
Job, C C	Mr	9 May 1914		1959 - 1984. Chair
Johnson, R	Mr	*	*	Pre 1896
Keeble, H	Mr	5 Nov 1841	2 Mar 1922	1874 - 1881; 1904 - 1917
Kemp, F	Mr	1909	*	Pre 1896
Kennard, S H	Mr, OBE	24 Mar 1909	21 Feb 1997	1962 - 1974. Chair
Knowles, T C	Mr	1845	1911	1888 - 189
Lamborn, H G	Mr, MP, MRSH, GLC	1 May 1915	21 Aug 1982	1965 - 1972
Lawson, A	Mr	*	*	Pre 1896
Leighton, H	Mrs	*	*	In period 1896 - 1920
Leighton, H T	Mrs	24 Feb 1872	*	1918 - 1920

Leighton, J S	Mr	2 May 1869	28 July 1948	1909 - 1912; 1914 - 1917
Lidbetter, W J	Mr, FRIBA	13 Jan 1931		1984 - 1985
Limbourne, F C	Mr	10 Nov 1910	*	1950 - 1952
Ling, W	Mr	1861	*	1922 -1923
Lingwood, H J	Mr	25 Nov 1906	14 Jun 1966	1954 - 1956
Lockyear, F	Mr	1860	*	1913 - 1923
Lucas, J	Mr	*	*	Pre 1896
Lumsden, J	Mr	*	*	Pre 1896
Machen, W J	Mr	26 Jul 1838	1922	Pre 1896
Mackay, R	Mr	1851	1902	1886 - 1894. Chair. 1898 - 1901
Maddox, H	Mr	*	*	Pre 1896
Marlow, W	Mr	*	*	Pre 1896
Mason, R I	Mr	11 Nov 1905	31 Jul 1967	1959 - 1965
May, H J	Mr	1867	19 Nov 1939	In period 1896 - 1920 Chair
McIntyre, I R	Mrs	1855	1920	In period 1896 - 1920
McLeod, A	Mr	29 Sep 1832	17 May 1902	1868. Founder
McQueen, A	Mr	*	*	Pre 1896
Mee, H	Mr	*	*	1868. Founder
Millar, G	Mr	*	*	Pre 1896. Chair
Mills, J	Mr	*	*	In period 1896 - 1920 Chair
Millward, T	Mr	*	*	1868. Founder

Moore, T	Mr	*	*	Pre 1896
Morrison, C	Mr	*	*	1868. Founder
Newell, W J	Mr	*	*	In period 1896 - 1920
Nicholson, G	Mr	*	*	Pre 1896
Norris, A E	Mr, JP	6 Dec 1917	10 May 1989	1978 - 1984
O'Brien, J	Mr	1862	*	In period 1896 - 1920. Chair
Oberman, A J	Mr, BA, PGCE	11 Jun 1943		1978 - 1985
Ogilvie, D	Mr	*	*	In period 1896 - 1920
Parsons, M	Mr	*	*	Pre 1896
Patterson, W	Mr	*	*	1868. Founder
Pearce, J	Mr	*	*	1868. Founder
Peeps, H	Mr	*	*	Pre 1896
Pickering, T	Mr	*	*	Pre 1896
Press, W	Mr	*	*	1868. Founder
Prior, A L	Mr, JP	16 April 1910	14 Dec 1973	1952 - 1973. Chair
Prudhoe, R	Mr	*	*	In period 1896 - 1920
Raggett, C S	Mr	10 Feb 1943		1975 - 1985
Read, J	Mr	*	*	From 1868. Founder. Chair
Real, E	Mrs	9 May 1875	7 May 1962	1923 - 1927
Reilly, J	Mr	*	*	Pre 1896
Reynolds, C H	Mr	*	*	1921
Ritchie, J	Mr	*	*	Pre 1896

Rose, W	Mr	1843	7 Mar 1931	1868. Founder
Ross, A	Mrs	*	1933	1920
Ryan, W	Mr	*	*	Pre 1896
Sandford, T	Mr	*	*	Pre 1896
Saunders, E G	Mr, JP	10 Feb 1880	28 Mar 1960	1927 - 1946
Seal, J	Mr	*	8 Feb 1919	From 1868. Founder
Sellicks, A	Mr	1845	1903	Pre 1896
Shaw, R	Mr	*	*	Pre 1896. Chair
Sheppard, J T	Mr, Cllr	1867	11 Apr 1949	1920. Chair
Short, J	Mr	*	*	Pre 1896
Shrive, C S	Mr	16 Jan 1933		1978 - 1985
Smith, T T	Mr	*	*	Pre 189
Smith, W	Mr	*	*	Pre 1896
Spurgeon, D A	Mr, BA	13 Aug 1926		1984 - 1985
Stafford, J	Mr	*	*	*. Chair
Steer, J	Mr	*	*	*
Styles, F W	Mr, BEM, Dip Ed, GLC	18 Dec 1914	June 1998	1968 - 1984. Chair
Sugar, J D	Mr	1877	29 May 1919	Pre 1919
Sutherland, G	Mr	3 Sept 1825	16 Oct 1904	1876 - 1896 Chair
Swanson, H	Mr	*	*	Pre 1896
Syer, T	Mr	*	*	Pre 1896
Sykes, H	Mr	1880	*	1921

Taylor, H	Mr	*	*	Pre 1896
Thacker, J	Mr	*	*	Pre 1896
Thomas, F A	Mr	*	*	c1920. Chair
Thresher, R	Mr	*	*	Pre 1896
Tommas, G G	Mr	*	*	Pre 1896
Tucker, M A	Mrs	28 Jan 1882	9 Mar 1947	1931 - 1947
Tuffield, T	Mr	*	*	Pre 1896
Turner, J	Mr	*	*	*
Unwin, L	Mrs	2 Feb 1917	7 Sep 1981	1959 - 1962
Veale, J	Mr	*	*	1868. Founder
Wale, R R	Mr	Jun 1862	11 Feb 1934	1896 - 1933. Chair
Wall, W T	Mr	1887	*	1925 - 1927
Wareham, S	Mr	*	*	1868. Founder
Wheeler, H	Mr	*	*	Pre 1896. Chair
Williams, T E	Lord, of Ynyshir	*	18 Feb 1966	1919 - 1923
Woodfield, G	Mr	*	*	Pre 1896

* No record available.

Service given to date of merger.

APPENDIX 2
SOUTH SUBURBAN CO-OPERATIVE SOCIETY MANAGEMENT COMMITTEE MEMBERS 1918 to 1984

NAME	TITLE	BORN	DIED	SERVICE
Aikman, J R	Mr	3 May 1911	*	1977 - 1980
Allonby, D L	Mr, JP, MSc. OBE	5 Feb 1933		1983-1984
Armstrong, W	Mr	*	*	1947 - 1950
Ash, E S A	Mrs	*	*	1946
Askew, F H	Mr	25 Jul 1926		1983 - 1984
Atkins, G A	Mr	*	*	1956 - 1970. President
Bacon, E J	Mr	23 Oct 1919	*	1983 - 1984
Bailey, C	Mr	1859	Nov 1942	1918 - 1938. President
Baldwin, M M	Mrs, JP, BA	8 Apr 1925	*	1983-1984
Ball, C J	Mr	23 May 1924	*	1977 - 1980
Ballard, M A	Mrs	*	*	1918 - 1919
Barnes, C E	Mr	*	*	1950 - 1954
Barnes, F C	Mr	*	*	1954 - 1961
Beggs, F J H	Mr	14 May 1915	*	1978 - 80
Bolton, C A G	Mr	28 Sept 1918	*	1979 - 1980
Bowden, A E G	Mr	*	*	1961 - 1967

Brett, L	Mrs	*	*	1953 - 1964
Brown, W J	Mr	*	*	1948 - 1957; 1960 - 1963
Burbage, L V	Mr	*		1950 -19 61; 1969 - 1975
Buttle, J F R	Mr, JP	*	*	1927 - 1949. President
Byrne, M F	Mrs	*	*	1974 - 1977
Cameron, D A	Mrs	11 Mar 1930	*	1974 - 84
Cane, H C	Mr	* 1957 - 1974.	*	1953 - 1954;
Clarke, S G	Mr, MBE	*	*	1946 - 1966. President
Constable, W J	Mr	*	*	1950 - 1954; 1957- 1958
Coombes, A E	Mr	*	*	1950 - 1952
Cooper, D W	Mr	*	1928	1922 - 1926
Coster, J	Mrs	21 Aug 1947	*	1983 - 1984
Cranfield, D A	Mrs	*	*	1942 - 1947
Crimp, N E	Mrs	*	*	1949
Cullen, A E	Mr	1 Jan 1914	Nov 1982	1967 - 1980. President
Dale, W F	Mr	*	*	1919 - 1937
Davis, W	Mr	*	1943	1918 - 1943
Drummond, W	Mr	*	*	1918 - 1942
England, K H	Mrs	*	*	1958 - 1961
Excell, G H	Mr	*	*	1973 - 1977
Field, M A P	Mr	14 Jun 1941	*	1983 - 1984

Filbey, J R F	Mrs	*	*	1948 - 1954
Flockhart, H V	Mr	*	*	1953 - 1959
Fooks, L W	Mr	*	*	1918 - 1926
Fuller, S	Mrs	*	*	1944 - 1945
Gale, B G	Mr	29 Dec 1914	*	1980 - 1984
Gibson, L C	Mr	*	*	1967
Gore, A	Mr	*	*	1918 - 1945
Hamer, A	Mrs	*	*	1937 - 1950
Hamer, P W	Mr	*	*	1936
Hancock, H C	Mr	*	1974	1962 - 1973
Harding, P W	Mr	*	*	1933 - 1964
Heaton, C	Mrs, JP	*	*	1926 - 1932
Heaton, W J	Mr	*	*	1923 - 1925
Holton, H	Mr	*	*	1938 - 1941
Jackson, D	Mr	*	*	1978 - 1980
Jarrett, S	Mr	*		1984
Jones, H C	Mr	*	*	1933 - 1946
Joy, K L	Mr, AAAI, AMinstCM	*		1977 - 1980
Keane, B	Mr	*	*	1965 - 1972. President
Keen, J	Mr, CHD	*	*	1922 - 1937
Kirman, B H	Dr	*	*	1941
Knight, F R	Mr	*	*	1956 - 1966

Koch, J K	Mr	*	1936	1918 - 1935
Laithwaite, M L	Mrs	*	*	1958 - 1966
Langdon, F	Mr	*	*	1946 - 1948
Latham, W	Mr	*	*	1968 - 1972
Lee, C W	Mr	*	*	1948
Lewis, W E	Mr	*	*	1952 - 1953
Lord, F	Mr	*	*	1918 - 1941 President
Loveman, A I	Mrs	*	*	1957 - 1958
Madgwick, E	Mr	*	*	1920 - 1925
Mason, T J	Mr	*	*	1936 - 1945
McArdle, N	Mr	2 Mar 1947	*	1977 - 1978
Mileham, E G	Mr	*	*	1956 - 1960
Miles, R	Mr	*	*	1928 - 1947
Moodey, J S	Mr	4 Jan 1914	*	1983 - 1984
Nealon, C	Mrs, JP	*	*	1930 - 1932
Newman, H E	Mr	*	*	1952- 1953
Newton, A E	Mr	*	*	1944 - 1972
O'Leary, A W	Mr	*	*	1980
Owen, W J	Mr, MP	*	*	1961 - 1969. President
Pamment, J	Mr	*	*	1918 - 1920
Pearce, E A C	Mr	11 Sep 1909	*	1967 - 1979
Pearce, L	Mrs	*	*	1969 - 1977

Penfold, H	Mr	*	*	1924 - 1929
Pichowski, H T J	Mr	9 Jun 1919		1977 - 1984. President
Powell, C M	Mr	*	*	1958 - 1977. President
Rankin, A W	Mr	*	*	1918 - 1946
Rimer, P W	Mr	*	*	1967
Rodford, E J	Mr	6 Apr 1917	*	1983 - 1984
Rouse, A	Mrs	*	*	1926 - 1927
Rouse, W J	Mr	*	*	1924 - 1925
Schofield, D	Mrs	*	*	1965 - 1969
Sheldrake, E	Mr	12 Dec 1915	*	1983 - 1984
Short, F C	Mr	*	*	1960 - 1963
Skelton, L E	Mr	*	*	1963 - 1966
Smith, A W	Mr	*	*	1944 - 1950
Springate, R F	Mrs	*	*	1940 - 1954
Stewart, W Max	Mr	*	*	1974 - 1977
Stewart, William M	Mr	*	*	1918 - 1920
Stockford, M T	Mr, B Sc, MIEE, C Eng	29 Jul 1924	*	1983 - 1984
Taylor, M C	Mr	*	*	1968
Vousden, D W	Mr	*	*	1948 - 1950
Wade, G J	Mr	*	*	1918 - 1919
Walker, J L	Mr	30 Mar 1914	*	1971 - 1979. President

Webb, A A	Mrs	*	*	1919 - 1932
Wheal, H W J	Mr	*	*	1972 - 1977
White, C C	Mr	*	*	1942 - 1961. President
White, R L R	Mr	12 Aug 1920	*	1975 - 1980
Williams, L S R	Mr	*	*	1984
Winter, J V	Mr	9 Jun 1916	*	1963 - 1980
Wrigglesworth, I	Mr	*	*	1971 - 1973

* No record available.

Service given to date of merger.

158

APPENDIX 3

FORMER SOCIETIES IN RACS AND SSCS AREAS

The following societies are known to have existed in the trading areas of the former Royal Arsenal and South Suburban Societies. They have been listed in retail and productive sections.

RETAIL SOCIETIES

1	Sheerness Economical and Industrial Co-operative Society	1816 - 1919
2	Sheerness Co-operative Society	1849 - 1919
3	Croydon Co-operative Industrial Society	1859 - 1874
4	Woolwich & Plumstead Co-operative Society	1861 - 1863
5	Rotherhithe Co-operative & Industrial Society	1862 - 1862
6	South London Equitable & Industrial Society	1862 - 1863
7	Woolwich Co-operative & Provident Society	1862 - 1869
8	Norwood United Industrial Co-operative Society	1862 - 1870
9	Mitcham & Beddington Co-operative Industrial Society	
10	Belmont Amicable Society	1862 - 1872
11	Deptford Industrial Co-operative Provision Society	1862 - 1872
12	Brixton Co-operative Industrial & Provident Society	1862 - 1902
13	First Upper Norwood Industrial & Provident Co-operative Society	1863 - 1864
14	Reigate Industrial Co-operative Society	1863 - 1930

15	South Norwood Industrial Co-operative Society	1864 - 1866
16	Penge Industrial Co-operative Society	1864 - 1869
17	Brixton Result Co-operative Society	1864 - 1911
18	Bermondsey Industrial Co-operative Society	1865 - 1871
19	Forest Hill & Sydenham Co-operative Butchers Society	
20	Guildford Industrial Co-operative Society	1866 - 1869
21	South London Co-operative Industrial Provident Society	
22	North Woolwich & Silvertown Co-operative Society	1866 - 1871
23	Tonbridge Industrial Co-operative Society	1866 - 1872
24	Lewisham & Lee Industrial Co-operative Provision Society	
25	Bromley & West Kent Co-operative Society	1867 - 1869
26	Sunningdale Co-operative Industrial Provident Society	
27	Southwark Co-operative Provident & Industrial Society	
28	Sutton Industrial Co-operative Society	1868 - 1869
29	Rotherhithe & Bermondsey Co-operative Industrial Society	
30	Camberwell Co-operative Provident & Industrial Society	
31	Norwood, Anerley & Penge Co-operative Society	1868 - 1872
32	Greenwich Co-operative Industrial Society	1868 - 1872
33	South London Industrial Provision Society	1868 - 1872
34	Lambeth Co-operative Industrial Society	1868 - 1872
35	Royal Arsenal Co-operative Society	1868 - 1985

36	Beckenham Industrial Co-operative Society	1869 - 1872
37	Crays Industrial Co-operative Society	1870 - 1908
38	Balham Industrial Co-operative Society	1871 - 1895
39	Bermondsey Industrial Co-operative Society	1873 - 1874
40	Norwood Equitable Co-operative Society	1873 - 1879
41	East Surrey Co-operative Society	1873 - 1896
42	Faversham & Thanet Co-operative Society	1874 - 1969
43	Sittingbourne Co-operative Society	1874 - 1988
44	Sydenham Equitable Co-operative Society	1875 - 1877
45	Caterham Industrial Co-operative Society	1875 - 1906
46	Shoreham Co-operative Society	1876 - 1880
47	Kent Industrial Co-operative Society (Sundridge)	1876 - 1881
48	Redhill Union Co-operative Society	1877 - 1880
49	South London & General Co-operative Society	1978 - 1914
50	Hampton & New Hampton Co-operative Society	1879 - 1914
51	Penge & Beckenham Co-operative Society	1879 - 1918
52	Silvertown Co-operative Society	1881 - 1884
53	Bermondsey Industrial Co-operative Society	1881 - 1894
54	Addington Co-operative Society	1881 - 1921
55	West Greenwich Co-operative Society	1882 - 1898
56	Bromley Industrial Co-operative Society	1882 - 1918

57	Chislehurst Co-operative Society	1884 - 1893
58	Gravesend Co-operative Society	1884 - 1968
59	Lewisham Co-operative Society	1885 - 1893
60	Southwark Equitable Society	1885 - 1893
61	South East London Industrial Co-operative Society	1885 - 1909
62	Camberwell Industrial Co-operative	1886 - 1889
63	Tooting & Earlsfield Co-operative Society	1886 - 1892
64	East Greenwich Co-operative Society	1887 - 1904
65	Bexleyheath Co-operative Society	1887 - 1906
66	Croydon Industrial Co-operative Society	1887 - 1918
67	Wimbledon & Merton Co-operative Society	1888 - 1905
68	Norwood Co-operative Society	1889 - 1911
69	Epsom Co-operative Society	1889 - 1911
70	Cliffe at Hoo Co-operative Society	1889 - 1917
71	Guildford & District Co-operative Society	1891 - 1971
72	Woolwich & Plumstead Mutual Co-operative Society	1892 - 1893
73	Sutton Co-operative Society	1892 - 1897
74	Slough & District Co-operative Society	1892 - 1968
75	Sutton & District Industrial & Provident Co-operative Society	1893 - 1915
76	Camberwell & Peckham Co-operative & Industrial Society	1894 - 1903
77	Sevenoaks Co-operative Industrial & Provident Society	1894 - 1912

78	Tonbridge Co-operative Society	1897 - 1938
79	Godalming & District Co-operative Society	1897 - 1963
80	New Cross & Deptford Industrial Co-operative Society	1899 - 1902
81	Epsom Co-operative Society	1899 - 1916
82	Woking Co-operative Society	1899 - 1962
83	Addlestone & District Co-operative Society	1902 - 1962
84	Haslemere & District Co-operative Society	1903 - 1965
85	Edenbridge Co-operative Society	1905 - 1911
86	Walworth & District Co-operative Society	1906 - 1908
87	Bromley & Crays Co-operative Society	1908 - 1918
88	Sutton District Co-operative Society	1909 - 1915
89	Imperial Co-operative Society (Woolwich)	1909 - 1921
90	South Suburban Co-operative Society	1918 - 1984
91	New Charlton Economical Society	1847 - N/A
92	Redhill Industrial Co-operative Society	1863 - N/A
93	East Surrey Industrial & Provident Co-operative Society (Bermondsey)	1864 - N/A
94	Northfleet Industrial & Provident Society	1865 - N/A
95	Wandsworth Co-operative Society	1867 - N/A
96	Bromley & West End Co-operative Society	1867 - N/A
97	Hatcham Equitable Industrial & Provident Co-operative Society	1867 - N/A
98	South Metropolitan Independent Co-operative Society (Bermondsey)	1867 - N/A

99	Reliance Co-operative Industrial & Provident Society	1867 - N/A
100	Southern Districts Industrial Co-operative Society (Blackfriars)	1868 - N/A
101	Brixton Industrial & Provident Society Stores	1888 - N/A
102	West London Industrial Co-operative Society	1893 - N/A
103	Grove Co-operative Society (Deptford)	1908 - N/A
104	Surbiton Co-operative Society	N/A - 1912
105	Cobham Co-operative Society	N/A - 1914
106	Leathehead Co-operative Society	1893 - 1916
107	Horsham Co-operative Society	N/A - 1921
108	Sunningdale Co-operative Society	N/A - 1922
109	Dorking Co-operative Society	1921 - 1925
110	Greenstreet Co-operative Society	1877 - 1928
111	Thanet Co-operative Society	N/A - 1933
112	Sheerness & District Economical Society	1919 - 1970

PRODUCTIVE SOCIETIES

113	Bromley Co-operative Builders	N/A - 1895
114	Woolwich Baking Society	1826 - N/A
115	Co-operative Coal Society (Woolwich)	1845 - N/A
116	Co-operative Bacon Society (Woolwich)	1850c - N/A
117	Greenacre Society (Woolwich)	1850c - N/A

118	Woolwich Co-operative Provident Society	1851 - 1869
119	Atlas Iron Works Company (Southwark)	1852 - N/A
120	Block Printers Industrial Society (Merton)	1852 - N/A
121	Woolwich and Plumstead Society	1861 - 1865c
122	Agricultural and Horticultural Society	1867 - N/A
123	East Surrey Baking Society	1873 - N/A
124	Brixton Builders Co-operative Society	1878 - 1908
125	People's Society	1885 - 1888
126	Norwood Gardeners Society	1885 - 1912
127	Co-operative Dress and Mantle Makers (Walworth)	1889 - N/A
128	London Co-operative Leather Manufacturers Society	1891 - N/A
129	General Engineers Ltd (Lambeth)	1894 - N/A
130	Deptford Perseverance Society	1896 - N/A

APPENDIX 4
SHOPS AND MERGERS

This appendix summarises the merger history of the societies in four sections:

Section 1   Dates of mergers.

Section 2   Stores owned by societies at the time of their merger with the RACS.

Section 3   Stores owned by the SSCS at the time of its merger with the CWS.

Section 4   Stores owned by the RACS at the time of its merger with the CWS.

SECTION 1
DATES OF MERGERS

The retail co-operative societies in the south east of England that had merged with the CWS by February 1985, included many small societies that had at an earlier date merged into the Royal Arsenal or South Surburban Societies. These societies are listed below.

A   SOUTH SUBURBAN CO-OPERATIVE SOCIETY

The South Suburban Co-operative Society merged with the CWS on 28th July 1984.

It was originally formed in 1918 by the joining together of three co-operative societies:

BROMLEY AND CRAYS
Founded July 1908 from merger of Bromley Society (formed 1882) and
Crays Society (formed 1870).

CROYDON
Founded 1887.

PENGE AND BECKENHAM
Founded April 1879.

Later, two more societies merged with the South Suburban Society:

REIGATE
Merged in 1930.

TONBRIDGE
Merged in 1938.

B   ROYAL ARSENAL CO-OPERATIVE SOCIETY

The Royal Arsenal Co-operative Society merged with CWS on 9th February 1985. It was originally formed in 1868, under the name Royal Arsenal Supply Association, and changed in 1872 to the familiar name.

Other societies subsequently merged with it as listed below:

1   ADDLESTONE
Founded 1902. Joined by Cobham Society in 1912.
Merged with RACS on 14th September 1968.

2   EAST GREENWICH
Merged with RACS in June 1904.

3   FAVERSHAM AND THANET
Faversham founded in 1874. Isle of Thanet Society merged with it in 1933, resulting in name change. Merged with RACS on 21st July 1969.

4   GODALMING
Founded 1897. Merged with RACS on 20th July 1963.

5   GRAVESEND
Founded 1884 as Borough of Gravesend Society. In 1917 Cliffe at Hoo Society merged with it. In 1962 changed name to Gravesend Society.
Merged with RACS on 20th May 1968.

6   GUILDFORD
Founded 1891. Leatherhead Society merged in 1916; Horsham in 1921; Dorking in 1925. Gomshall, Cranleigh and Bookham Societies all also merged with Guildford. Merged with RACS on 25th January 1971.

7   HASLEMERE
Founded 1903. Merged with RACS on 19th July 1965.

8   SHEERNESS
Sheerness Economical Society was founded in 1816. Followed by Sheerness
Co-operative Society in 1849. The two societies merged in 1919.
Merged with RACS on 19th September 1970.

9   SLOUGH
Founded 1892. Acquired four shops from Reading Society in 1965.
Merged with RACS on 22nd July 1968.

10   SOUTH LONDON & GENERAL
Merged with RACS in 1913.

11   WALWORTH
Merged with RACS in 1908.

12   WOKING
Founded 1899 as Woking and Horsell Society. Changed name first c1905, then again
c1920 to Woking Society. Took over territory of Surbiton Society in 1912 when the
latter ceased trading. In 1922 Sunningdale Society and later the Camberley branch
of the Aldershot Society ceased to trade, and the Woking Society developed in
these areas. Merged with RACS on 1st September 1962.

SECTION 2

STORES OWNED BY SOCIETIES
AT TIME OF MERGER WITH RACS

Addlestone Co-operative Society

Addlestone (Registered office)	117 - 112	Station Road, Addlestone, Surrey.	Food & Non-food
Byfleet	140	High Road, Byfleet, Surrey.	Food & Hairdressing
Chertsey	66	Guildford Street, Chertsey, Surrey.	Food
Cobham	129	Anyards Road, Cobham, Surrey.	Food
Ottershaw	13	Brox Road, Ottershaw, Chertsey, Surrey.	Food

Walton	85 - 87	High Street,. Walton on Thames, Surrey.	Non-food
Walton	58 - 62	Terrace Road, Walton on Thames, Surrey.	Food & Hairdressing
Weybridge	9	High Street, Weybridge, Surrey.	Food & Electrical
Woodham	307	Woodham Lane, New Haw, Weybridge, Surrey.	Food & Hairdressing

East Greenwich Co-operative Society

Greenwich			Food

Faversham & Thanet Co-operative Society

Approach Road	65 & 67	Approach Road, Broadstairs, Kent.	Food
Beacon Road	27	Beacon Road, Broadstairs, Kent.	Food
Birchington	54-56	Station Road, Broadstairs, Kent.	Food
Broadstairs	56	St Peters Park Road, Broadstairs, Kent.	Food
Bush Parade	112 - 114	Newington Road, Ramsgate, Kent.	Food
Garlinge	166 - 168	Canterbury Road, Garlinge, Margate, Kent.	Food
Grange Road	24	Grange Road, Ramsgate, Kent.	Butchery

Lower Road	114	Lower Road, Faversham, Kent.	Food
Margate	113 - 117	High Street, Margate, Kent.	Food & Non-food
Margate Road	160	Margate Road, Ramsgate, Kent.	Butchery
Minster, Thanet	51	High Street, Minster, Thanet.	Food
Newington Centre	4	The Centre, Newington Estate, Ramsgate, Kent.	Food
Preston Street (Registered office)	60-63	Preston Street, Faversham, Kent.	Food & Non-food
Ramsgate	128 - 132	High Street, Ramsgate, Kent.	Food
Ramsgate	69 - 73	King Street, Ramsgate, Kent.	Non-food
Ramsgate Road	109	Ramsgate Road, Margate, Kent.	Food & Post Office
St Mary's Road	52	St Mary's Road, Faversham, Kent.	Food
Swalecliffe		The Broadway, 76 Herne Bay Road, Swalecliffe, Kent.	Food
Tankerton	148	Tankerton Road, Tankerton, Kent.	Food & Drapery
West Street	72	West Street, Faversham, Kent.	Food
Westgate	2	Belmont Road, Westgate, Kent.	Food & Post Office
Whitstable	58 - 60	Oxford Street, Whitstable, Kent.	Food & Menswear

Godalming Co-operative Society

Chiddingfold		Woodside Road, Chiddingfold, Surrey.	Food
Elstead			Food
Farncombe	61-65	St Johns' Street, Farncombe, Surrey.	
Godalming (Registered office)	1 - 17	Bridge Street, Godalming, Surrey.	Food & Non-food
Witley		Wheeler Street, Witley, Surrey.	Food

Gravesend Co-operative Society

Cliffe		Station Road, Cliffe, Kent.	Food
Clock Tower Filling Station	139	Milton Road, Gravesend, Kent.	Garage
Denton	4	East Milton Road, Denton, Kent.	Food
Echo Square	6	Echo Square, Gravesend, Kent.	Food
Harmer Street (Registered office)	3 - 11	Harmer Street, Gravesend, Kent.	Food & Non-food
Kings Farm	141	Central Avenue, Gravesend, Kent.	Food
Knockhall	22	Knockhall Chase, Greenhithe, Kent.	Food
Lawrance Square	18	Lawrance Square, Northfleet, Kent.	Food

Meopham		Station Approach, Meopham, Kent.	Food
Milton Road	148	Milton Road, Gravesend, Kent.	Food & Non-food
New Road	74, 75, & 76	New Road, Gravesend, Kent.	Food & Non-food
Old Road West	180 - 182	Old Road West, Gravesend, Kent.	Food
Painters Ash	35	Denholm Road, Northfleet, Gravesend, Kent.	Food
Perry Street	2	Market Buildings, Perry Street, Northfleet.	Food
Rochester Road	204	Rochester Road, Chalk, Kent.	Food
Swanscombe	40	High Street, Galley Hill, Swanscombe, Kent.	Food
The Hive		The Hive, High Street, Northfleet, Kent.	Food
Waterdales	149	Waterdales, North Fleet, Kent.	Food
Whitehill Road	155	Whitehill Road, Gravesend, Kent.	Food
Wrotham Road	61	Wrotham Road, Gravesend, Kent.	Food

Guildford Co-operative Society

Bookham		Leatherhead Road, Great Bookham, Surrey.	Food
Cranleigh	23	High Street, Cranleigh, Surrey.	Food & Non-food

Dorking	33	South Street, Dorking, Surrey.	Food
Gomshall		Station Road, Gomshall, Surrey.	Food
Guildford (Registered office)		North Street/Haydon Place, Guildford, Surrey.	Food & Non-food
Hazel Avenue		Hazel Avenue, Guildford, Surrey.	Food & Post Office
Horsham	6	East Street, Horsham, Sussex.	Food & Non-food
Leatherhead	3	North Street, Leatherhead, Surrey.	Food & Non-food
Madrid Road	48	Madrid Road, Guildford, Surrey.	Food
Partridge Green		High Street, Partridge Green, Sussex.	Food & Post Office
Shalford	3 - 4	Kings' Road, Shalford, Guildford, Surrey.	Food
Southway	111	Southway, Guildford, Surrey.	Food
Stoughton Road	4	Stoughton Road, Guildford, Surrey.	Food
Woodbridge Hill	48	Woodbridge Hill, Guildford, Surrey.	Food
Worplesdon Road	127	Worplesdon Road, Guildford, Surrey.	Food

Haslemere Co-operative Society

Beacon Hill		Grove Road, Beacon Hill, Hindhead, Surrey.	Food & Non-food

Camelsdale		Camelsdale Road, Camelsdale, Haslemere, Surrey.	Food
Fernhurst		The Cross, Fernhurst, Haslemere, Surrey.	Food
Grayshott		Headley Road, Grayshott, Hindhead, Surrey.	Food
Haslemere Central (Registered office)		Wey Hill, Haslemere, Surrey.	Food & Non-food
Liphook		Headley Road, Liphook, Hants.	Food & Non-food
Petworth		Golden Square, Petworth, Sussex.	Food
Sunvale		Sunvale Avenue, Haslemere, Surrey.	Food

Sheerness Co-operative Society

Eastchurch	84	High Street, Eastchurch, Sheerness, Kent.	Food
Halfway	27	Halfway Road, Halfway, Minster, Sheerness, Kent.	Food
Marine Town	5	Richmond Street, Sheerness, Kent.	Food
Minster, Sheerness	19 - 23	Queens Road, Minster, Sheerness, Kent.	Food & Hairdressing
Queenborough	1 - 3	Main Road, Queenborough, Isle of Sheppey, Kent.	Food
Sheerness Broadway	1, 11	The Broadway, Sheerness, Kent.	Non-food
Sheerness High Street (Registered office)	110 - 116	High Street, Sheerness, Kent.	Food & Non-food

St George's Avenue	179	St Georges Avenue, Sheerness, Kent.	Food
Victoria Street	33	Victoria Street, Sheerness, Kent.	Food

Slough Co-operative Society

Baylis Parade	7 - 9	Baylis Parade, Stoke Poges Lane, Slough, Berks.	Food
Burnham	94 - 96	High Street, Burnham, Berks.	Food
Burnham Lane	158	Burnham Lane, Slough, Berks.	Food
Chalvey		Chalvey Road, Slough, Berks.	Food
Cippenham	428	Bath Road, Cippenham, Berks.	Food
Dedworth Road	67	Dedworth Road, Windsor, Berks.	Food
Farnham Road	201 - 203	Farnham Road, Slough, Berks.	Food
Iver	37	High Street, Iver, Berks.	Food
Langley	250 - 252	High Street, Langley, Slough, Berks.	Food & Hair-dressing
Manor Park	6	Villiers Road, Manor Park, Slough, Berks.	Food
Old Windsor	6	Lyndwood Parade, St Luke's Road, Old Windsor, Berks.	Food
Salt Hill	121 & 130	Bath Road, Salt Hill, Slough, Berks.	Food

Slough Store (Registered office)	190 - 192	High Street, Slough, Berks.	Food & Non-food
Stoke Poges		Bell's Hill, Stoke Poges, Bucks.	Food
Stoke Road		Stoke Road, Slough, Berks.	Food
Trelawney Avenue	238 - 240	Trelawney Avenue, Slough, Berks.	Food
Wentworth Avenue	63 - 67	Wentworth Avenue, Farnham Royal, Slough, Berks.	Food
Wexham Road		Upton Lea Parade, Wexham Road, Slough, Berks.	Food

South London & General Co-operative Society

Lambeth		Viceroy Road, Lambeth SW8.	Food

Walworth Co-operative Society

Walworth		Walworth Road.	Food

Woking Co-operative Society

Camberley	53-56	London Road, Camberley, Surrey.	Food & Non-food
Claygate	17	Station Parade, Claygate, Surrey.	Food
Hersham	166	Hersham Road, Woking, Surrey.	Food
Horsell	111	High Street, Horsell, Woking, Surrey.	Food

Knaphill	26	High Street, Knaphill, Surrey.	Food
Lightwater		Guildford Road, Lightwater, Surrey.	Food
Maybury		Maybury Hill, Woking, Surrey.	Food
Old Woking	31	High Street, Old Woking, Surrey.	Food
Sheerwater	21	Dartmouth Avenue, Sheerwater, Surrey.	Food
Sunninghill		Bagshot Road, Sunninghill, Berks.	Food
Well Lane	62	Well Lane, Horsell, Woking, Surrey.	Food
Woking Store (Registered office)	45 & 47	Church Street/Percy Street, Woking, Surrey.	Food & Non-food

SECTION 3

SOUTH SUBURBAN SHOPS AS AT NOVEMBER 1984

Addington	7-8 Central Parade, New Addington, Surrey.	Food
Addiscombe	311 Lower Addiscombe Road, Addiscombe, Kent.	Food
Anerley	147 Anerley Road, Anerley, SE20.	Food
Bellingham	38-40 Randelsdown Road, Bellingham, SE6. 42-44 Randelsdown Road, Bellingham, SE6.	Food Butchery
Bromley	2 Chatterton Road, Bromley Common, Kent.	Food
Carshalton	386-390 Middleton Road, Carshalton, Surrey.	Food
Coulsdon	12-16 Chipstead Valley Road, Coulsdon, Surrey.	Food
Croydon	61 Lower Addiscombe Road, Croydon, Surrey.	Food

Downham	445-453 Bromley Road, Downham, Kent.	Food
	426 Downham Way, Downham, SE6.	Food
Edenbridge	58 High Street, Edenbridge, Kent.	Food
Eden Park	313-315 Upper Elmers End Road, Eden Park, Kent.	Food
Epsom	43-49 Tattenham Crescent, Epsom, Surrey.	Food
Hayes	22 Station Approach, Hayes, Kent.	Butchery
Penge	6 The Blenheim Centre, Clarina Road, Penge, Kent.	Superstore
Reigate	40 Allingham Road, South Park, Reigate, Surrey.	Food
	11-13 Woodhatch, Reigate, Surrey.	Food
St Pauls Cray	95-101 Cotmandene Crescent, St Pauls Cray, Kent.	Food
Sanderstead	347-351 Limpsfield Road, Hamsey Green, Surrey.	Food
Sevenoaks	1-2 Carlton Parade, St Johns Hill, Sevenoaks, Kent.	Food
Shirley	225-227 Wickham Road, Shirley, Surrey.	Food
Stoneleigh	34-36 The Broadway, Stoneleigh, Surrey.	Food
Streatham	107-111 Streatham Vale, Streatham, SW16.	Food
Sutton	62 London Road, Rosehill, Sutton, Surrey.	Food
	5-7 Stonecot Hill, Sutton, Surrey.	Food
Thornton Heath	722-728 London Road, Thornton Heath, Surrey.	Food
	26-28 Green Lane, Thornton Heath, Surrey.	Food
Wallington	64-66 Woodcote Road, Wallington, Surrey.	Butchery
Westerham	6 The Grange, High Street, Westerham, Kent.	Food
	Brunswick House, High Street, Westerham.	Non-food
West Norwood	294-296 Norwood Road, West Norwood, SE27.	Food
West Wickham	3-5 High Street, West Wickham, Kent.	Food
	42-46 Croydon Road, Coney Hall, West Wickham, Kent.	Food

ROYAL ARSENAL SHOPS AS AT JANUARY 1985

Abbey Wood	106-116 McLeod Road, Abbey Wood, SE2.	Food
Addlestone	117 Station Road, Addlestone, Surrey.	Superstore
Bexleyheath	131 The Broadway, Bexleyheath, Kent.	Food/H'maker
Bostall Heath	297-303 Brampton Road, Bexleyheath, Kent.	Food
Belvedere	21 Picardy Street, Belvedere, Kent.	Food
Birchington	56 Station Road, Birchington, Kent.	Food
Blackfen	7-11 Blackfen Parade, Blackfen Road, Sidcup, Kent.	Food
Blackheath	17 Old Dover Road, Blackheath, SE3.	Food
Brewery Road	15 Brewery Road, Plumstead, SE18.	Food
Brixton Hill	264-270 Brixton Hill, Brixton, SW2.	Food
Bush Parade	112-114 Newington Road, Ramsgate, Kent.	Food
Camberley	53-56 London Road, Camberley, Surrey.	Food/H'maker
Camberwell New Rd	177-183 Camberwell New Road, Camberwell, SE5.	Food
Charlton Village	19-23 The Village, Charlton, SE7.	Food
Chiddingfold	Woodside Road, Chiddingfold, Surrey.	Food
Cranleigh	23 High Street, Cranleigh, Surrey.	Food
East Greenwich	210-218 Trafalgar Road, Greenwich, SE10.	Food
Eltham	168-176 High Street, Eltham, SE9.	Food/H'maker
Erith	28-40 Pier Road, Erith, Kent.	Food
Evelyn Street	317-319 Evelyn Street, Deptford, SE8.	Food
Falconwood Park	21-23 Falconwood Park, Welling, Kent.	Food

Farncombe	61-65 St Johns' Street, Farncombe, Surrey.	Food
Faversham	60-63 Preston Street, Faversham, Kent.	Food/H'maker
Grand Drive	300 Grand Drive, Raynes Park, SW20.	Food
Grange Road	24 Grange Road, Ramsgate, Kent	Butchery
Grayshott	Headley Road, Grayshott, Hindhead, Surrey.	Food
Grovebury	34-38 Grovebury Road, Abbey Wood, SE2.	Food
Halfway	27 Halfway Road, Halfway, Minster, Sheerness, Kent.	Food
Haslemere	Lion Green, Shottermill, Haslemere, Surrey.	Food
Herbert Road	9-15 Herbert Road, Plumstead, SE18.	Food
Hersham	166 Hersham Road, Woking, Surrey.	Food
Hither Green	200-206 Hither Green Lane, Hither Green, SE13.	Food
Holburne Road	169-173 Holburne Road, Blackheath, SE3.	Food
Horsell	111, High Street, Horsell, Woking, Surrey.	Food
Kidbrooke Park	196-200 Shooters Hill Road, Blackheath, SE3.	Food
Knaphill	26 High Street, Knaphill, Surrey.	Food
Lakedale Road	18-30 Lakedale Road, Plumstead, SE18.	Food
Lambeth Walk	120-126 Lambeth Walk, Lambeth, SE11.	Food
Langley	250-252 High Street, Langley, Slough, Berks.	Food
Links	196-212 Plumstead Common Rd, Plumstead, SE18.	Food
Long Lane	131-135 Long Lane, Bexleyheath, Kent.	Food
Lordship Lane	111-115 Lordship Lane, East Dulwich, SE22.	Food
Milton Road	148 Milton Road, Gravesend, Kent.	Food

Minster	19-23 Queens Road, Minster, Sheerness, Kent.	Food
Mottingham	276-280 Court Road, Eltham, SE9.	Butchery
Motspur Park	350-352 West Barnes Lane, Motspur Park, SW20.	Food
New Cross Road	283-287 New Cross Road, New Cross, SE14.	Food
New Eltham	370-380 Footscray Road, New Eltham, SE9.	Food
Northumberland H'th	283-287, Bexley Road, Erith, Kent.	Food
Orpington	The Walnuts Centre, Homefield Rise, Orpington, Kent.	Superstore
Painters Ash	35 Denholm Road, Northfleet, Gravesend, Kent.	Food
Perry Street	14-18 Perry Street, Northfleet, Kent.	Food
Pickford Lane	4-12 Pickford Lane, Bexleyheath, Kent.	Food
Plough Green	384 Malden Road, Worcester Park, Surrey.	Food
Queenborough	1-3 Main Road, Queenborough, Isle of Sheppey, Kent.	Food
Raynes Park	8-12 Coombe Lane, Raynes Park, SW20.	Food
Sheerness	110-116 High Street, Sheerness, Kent.	Food/H'maker
Shooters Hill	428-430 Well Hall Road, Eltham, SE9.	Food
Slade Green	41-49 Forest Road, Slade Green, Erith, Kent.	Food
Southwark Park Road	192-221 Southwark Park Road, Southwark, SE16.	Food
Swalecliffe	The Broadway, 76 Herne Bay Road, Swalecliffe, Kent.	Food
Tolworth	26-34 Tolworth Broadway, Tolworth, Surrey.	Food
Tooting	180-214 Upper Tooting Road, Tooting, SW17.	Food
Tooting Junction	271-275 Mitcham Road, Tooting, SW17.	Food
Trelawney Avenue	238-240 Trelawney Avenue, Slough, Berks.	Food

Upper Belvedere	56-64 Nuxley Road, Upper Belvedere, Kent.	Food
Valliers Wood	188a Halfway Street, Sidcup, Kent.	Food
Walton	58-62 Terrace Road, Walton on Thames, Surrey.	Food
Walworth Road	371-373 Walworth Road, Walworth, SE 17.	Food/Hmaker
Well Hall	158-170 Well Hall Road, Eltham, SE 9.	Food
Welling	71-79 High Street, Welling, Kent.	Superstore
Wentworth Avenue	63-67 Wentworth Avenue, Farnham Royal, Berks.	Food
West Greenwich	229-235 Greenwich High Road, Greenwich, SE 10.	Food
Westhorne Avenue	546-550 Westhorne Avenue, Eltham, SE 9.	Food
Westwood	475 Margate Road, Broadstairs, Kent.	Superstore
Whitehill Road	155 Whitehill Road, Gravesend, Kent.	Food
Whitstable	58-60 Oxford Street, Whitstable, Kent.	Food
Wimbledon Chase	276-288 Kingston Road, Wimbledon, SW20.	Food
Wimbledon Park	173-177 Arthur Road, Wimbledon, SW19.	Food
Woking	45 Church Street West, Woking, Surrey.	Superstore
Woodbridge Hill	48 Woodbridge Hill, Guildford, Surrey.	Food
Woolwich	132-152 Powis Street, Woolwich, SE18.	Food/Hmaker

Nb. H'maker - Homemaker

APPENDIX 5
HOW PROPORTIONAL REPRESENTATION WORKED IN THE RACS

Introduction

The usual arrangement for the election of committees in retail co-operative societies in the UK is to adopt the 'first past the post' system by use of the cross vote.

However, the Norwest and Royal Arsenal Societies used the Single Transferable Voting System of Proportional Representation in their elections. Royal Arsenal adopted the system in 1921 and used it to elect its General, Education, and Political Purposes Committees along with its delegates to Co-operative Congress. The cross vote system was used in electing delegates to CWS meetings and scrutineers.

Following the merger with the CWS in February 1985, the system continued to be used in the elections for Branch Committees until 1994. This arrangement was then discontinued in favour of the cross vote.

There are several variations of PR, and none is easily explained in a few words. However, the following information was prepared to help members to understand the basic principles involved. The precise regulations were contained in the RACS Rule Book and subsequently in CWS Branch Committee standing orders.

The Member Relations Department arranged practical voting demonstrations on request from groups of members, to explain how the system worked.

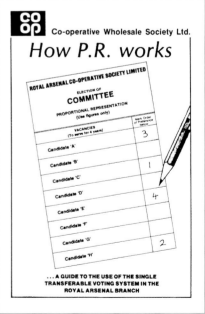

How to Vote

Members must mark on the ballot paper the figure 1 opposite the name of the candidate of their first choice and indicate the order of their preference for as many candidates as they wished by placing against the candidates' names the figure 2, 3, 4, 5 and so on. If, for instance, there are 30 candidates for 12 vacancies, members may, if they wish, vote for all 30 or just one.

It will be seen that numbers are used in place of the normal 'X'. This enables the Returning Officer to transfer the vote to the member's next choice if their first and subsequent preferences are elected or eliminated as the count progresses.

Counting the Papers

The ballot papers are removed from the ballot boxes, counted and the total number of votes cast is recorded. Those papers that are spoiled are removed, leaving only the valid votes.

The Quota

To arrive at the quota, the Returning Officer divides the total number of valid votes cast by the number of vacancies to be filled plus 1 and, ignoring any fractions, adds one to the result. For example, if 2643 valid votes were cast in an election for twelve vacancies, the quota would be 2643 divided by 13, which equals 203 (ignoring the fraction), plus 1 = 204.

The First Count

The ballot papers are sorted according to the first preferences (the number 1's) cast for each candidate. Any candidate who obtains the quota is declared elected.

The Surplus and its Transfer

A surplus arises when candidates obtain more votes than the quota. When this happens the surplus votes of the elected candidate(s) are transferred to the second preference candidates (number 2's) in proportion to the size of the surplus itself. For example, if the quota was 204 and the elected candidate had 272 first preferences, all the 272 papers would be re-sorted among the second preferences. After re-sorting, each second preference candidate would receive as votes one quarter of the number of papers credited to him because the surplus (68) was one-quarter of the total number of first preference votes cast (273). On the second and subsequent counts, only those votes which actually produce a candidate's surplus are taken into account.

Exclusion of Candidates

If no candidate reaches the quota on the first or subsequent counts, the one with the lowest number of votes is eliminated from the poll. This is done by examining all his or her papers and transferring the votes to the remaining non-elected candidates for whom the next preferences are recorded.

If, at any stage, two candidates tie with the lowest number of votes, the one who recorded the lowest number of first preferences at the first count is eliminated first.

Non-transferable Votes

As the count progresses, it is possible that the number of preferences indicated on a ballot paper becomes exhausted e.g. a member may have voted for only three candidates, each of whom has already been elected or eliminated. In such a case, the ballot paper becomes non-transferable and cannot be used in any subsequent counts.

Conclusion of the Count

The procedure of elimination and transfer is continued until one more candidate than the number of vacancies to be filled remains. The lowest placed candidate, i.e. the thirteenth, then becomes the next continuing candidate, or runner-up, and the others (whether or not they have reached the quota) are elected. The status of the next continuing candidate is important as, in certain circumstances, the Returning Officer may return him or her to fill a casual vacancy that may occur at a later date.

A good practical example of how the system works is seen in the following detailed result of an election. It will be noted that, while candidate 'C' was placed fifth with 405 votes on the first count, he or she nonetheless failed to secure election, whereas candidate 'R', placed ninth with 293 votes on the first count, was eventually elected in the fifth place.

EXAMPLE OF AN ELECTION

Number of papers issued 6, 118; Papaers spoiled 131; No. of valid votes 5,987; No. of seats 7; Quota 748 + 1 = 749

CANDI-DATES	1ST COUNT	COUNTS 2 TO 14 — TRANSFER OF SURPLUS VOTES													RESULT	FINAL POSITION
		J+	W	N	M	G	P	S+	T	F	D	V	E	L		
A	644	+3	+2	+8	+21	+13	+7	+2	+33	+14	+26				773	Elected 3rd - A
B	341	+3		+6	+4	+5	+6		+14	+13	+12	+70	+108	+34	616	Elected 6th - B
C	405	+1	+1	+1	+3	+2	+2	+1	+1	+13	+11	+18	+15	+38	511	Next continuing - C
D	147	+14	+28	+5	+1		+10	+1	+3	+29	-238					
E	280	+1	+1	+8	+4	+13	+16	+2	+1	+9	+4	+45	-383			
F	165	+1	+1	+2		+4	+17	+2	+6	-197						
G	98	+2		+2	+8	-112										
H	622	+3	+1	+3	+2	+4	+3	+1	+2	+55	+22	+8	+18	+24	767	Elected 4th - H
J	964	-215													749	Elected 1st - J
K	324	+2	+1	+1	+2	+2	+3	+1	+12	+15	+10	+42	+44	+124	582	Elected 7th - K
L	359	+2		+2	+1	+3	+3	+1	+2	+16	+11	+16	+14	-430		
M	86		+1	+1	-88											
N	81	+1	+1	-83												
P	114	+1		+4	+4	+8	-131									
R	293	+175		+5	+2	+3	+19	+2	+10	+8	+75	+27	+32	+36	689	Elected 5th - R
S	687	+5		+15	+7	+26	+24	-16							749	Elected 2nd - S
T	171	+2	+3	+3		+1	+4	+1	-182							
V	169	+1		+4	+6	+1	+4	+3	+84	+10	+9	-291				
W	37		-37													
Non-trans*			+1	+13	+19	+27	+13		+14	+15	+58	+65	+152	+174	551	
	5987														5987	

*Non-transferable papers   +Surplus

APPENDIX 6
DIVIDEND IN THE ROYAL ARSENAL CO-OPERATIVE SOCIETY LTD

Introduction

Retail co-operative societies throughout the UK adopted various systems to distribute their profits to members in proportion to their purchases. In 1881 and 1892, two special national committees were set up to review the systems being used by societies and to make recommendations as to the best one to use. Some used metallic or tin checks, others used a paper system combined with metal checks, or kept records in ledgers, or used a paper system known as the 'Climax' system, which was the one recommended by the 1892 committee. The Royal Arsenal Society used the metal check system.

Metal Checks

Early balance sheets of the RACS reveal that members had to exchange their bills for one pound checks. It was not until May 1875 that mention was made of tin checks. The tokens were made in denominations of £1, £2, and £5 and were commonly called 'tin checks' and 'brass checks'. The tokens were issued to the value of the purchase made.

At the conclusion of each trading half year, members deposited their checks with the Society and the total value of their purchases thus obtained was recorded against their memberships number. The disposable profit or surplus was divided by the total purchases and members were then notified of how much dividend was due to them based on the number of pounds deposited in tokens. The member could either withdraw the dividend in cash or have it added to their share account.

Payment of Dividend

In spite of a long period of depression following the end of the South African War in 1901, the Society expanded its area of operations, primarily through mergers, and with this expansion came an increase in membership. As a result, changes were introduced in 1913 to the method by which the Society's half-yearly dividend and interest were paid. They aimed to reduce labour, by introducing a more flexible system that allowed the dividend to be paid simultaneously at Woolwich and in other areas, with greater speed of payment.

The new system involved the issuing of a new form of receipt which was issued when share pass books were presented at branches for making up.

The receipt was in two parts, 'A' and 'B'. The 'A' portion was a receipt for the share pass book, and the 'B' portion a check receipt and dividend payment voucher. Members wishing to withdraw their dividend on the specified dates presented the 'B' portion, duly completed, to the payment clerk at the shop where they deposited their checks. Payment would be made and the share pass book and cancelled receipt returned to the member.

Members not wishing to withdraw their dividend had to wait one week after the three days of dividend paying before they could collect their share pass books duly made up to date.

Some of the wider implications of the dividend system, involving rationing and taxation, have been mentioned in Chapter 5.

Special Bakery Dividend

In 1909 local bakers were giving special discounts on bread which brought about a decrease in the Society's bread trade.

To meet this competition and attract new members it was agreed to change the Society's rules to allow differential dividends to be paid. As a result, bread and flour sold from vans had a different tin check system carrying with it a higher dividend, whilst the existing system operated for goods sold in shops. Special metal bakery checks were issued which could be exchanged for brass tokens of five shillings (25p) and 20 shillings (£1)

New employees visiting check distributing office at Commonwealth Buildings, Woolwich

which were accepted each half-year when checks were returned. The new checks began to be issued on 5th May 1909. For the first few half years, a special bread dividend of two shillings (10p) to members and one shilling to non-members was paid.

The arrangement ceased on January 1917, when the Society's bakery sales were over £750,000, and its termination was brought about by difficulties created in World War I. Supplies of metal checks were unreliable because metal was required for the war effort; and the trained labour required to maintain separate bakery records, had left for Government work. From the 15th January, 1917, metal checks of each type were issued for all purposes, and bakery brass tokens of five shillings (25p) were handed in with other brass checks and dividend paid on multiples of £1.

Trafficking

In the mid-1930s, it was apparent that there was a considerable amount of trafficking in the Society's checks. Small shopkeepers and others were exploiting the needs of members who, finding themselves in temporary financial difficulties, were prepared to dispose of their checks at a figure considerably less than they would have received if they had waited until dividend was paid.

The Society's rule relating to the allocation of surplus was not legally watertight to prevent the assignment of checks, a situation that became clear when a court case was decided against the Society.

In an effort to stop this trafficking, the Society introduced the payment of an interim dividend, which was followed in June 1939 by a change to rule which gave the Society power to withhold dividend on any checks returned which did not represent the purchases of the member returning them.

Interim Dividend

As outlined in the preceding paragraph, there were indications that many members would welcome the opportunity, when the necessity arose, to receive an interim dividend on the checks they had in hand before the usual dividend paying periods. Accordingly, arrangements were made in October/November 1935 - when purchases of winter clothing, footwear and household requirements (coal) were being made - for members to exchange not less than £5 in brass checks at any of the five principal district offices at Woolwich, Lewisham, Peckham, Walworth and Tooting, and obtain in exchange vouchers which entitled them to obtain goods to the value of the dividend allowed, in any dry goods shop. Dividend was 1s 6d (7½p) in the pound at that time, and interim vouchers exchanged qualified for death benefit. Members did not sacrifice the usual advantages of membership.

The scheme was remarkably successful and continued until the outbreak of World War II.

Check Distributing Office

Some idea of the work necessary in the Society's check distributing office at Commonwealth Buildings to verify returns from each branch check office, was recounted in the November 1939 edition of the Society's staff magazine *Together*. The article described how the 'check office girls' sorted the various denominations of checks into sorting bins:

These sorting bins are on tables ranged in rows up and down the spacious room. At each bin sit two girls, and the speed at which they sort the checks into the nine divisions has to be seen to be believed...

Other girls sit at benches round the walls and count the sorted checks, making them up into parcels of 500 – also at speed. These parcels are then packed tightly into strong wood or metal boxes, padlocked and sealed with the number of the branch to which the box is going.

At the end of each half year about 40 tons of tin checks come in. These cannot be sorted at once but are worked in with the normal weekly sorting.

Every Thursday the Check Sorting Office sends out 250 tightly packed boxes. Each box contains 1 cwt of sorted checks, equal to £1,000 denominational value – i.e. checks for £1,000 worth of purchases. Each £1,000 worth of assorted checks averages out at 23,000 checks.

When there is a big shopping event on, such as a Dividend Sale, they have to send a lot more of course.

There are 75 girls in the Check Sorting Office at Commonwealth Buildings, and approximately 450 Check Office girls at the branches.

Every girl in the Sorting Office can sort £100's worth (ie 2,300) mixed checks per hour – comfortably. Some of them can do a lot more.

Climax Check System

On 25th January 1960, tin and brass checks ceased to be given. Instead a 'Climax' check was given, the purpose of which was to check the cash received by shop assistants and enable each member's purchases to be ascertained for dividend purposes. Details of an earlier experiment with this system are included in chapter 3.

The membership number, the amount of sale and other particulars were entered on the check at the time that the transaction was made, although not every department issued checks, e.g. catering, funerals and memorials, travel, coaches, etc. The entries were consecutively numbered and made in triplicate. One copy was given to the member when the cash was received. The sales assistants paid in their cash daily to the shop managers, supported by a paying-in slip and the duplicate copy of the climax check. The third copy remained at the branch. The checks were then totalled to ascertain total sales, check assistants' 'overs' and 'shorts', and to accumulate each members' purchases for the accounting period.

Members were expected to see that the correct membership number and amount of the purchase were recorded on each check, and to retain and total them in order that they could verify the amount of purchases credited on their dividend warrant by the office at the end of each trading period.

This system was operated by the Society until 1970.

Dividend Stamp Scheme

The Co-operative Dividend Stamp Scheme was introduced by the CWS in 1968 but did not commence in the Society until 7th September 1970. From this date, membership numbers were no longer recorded when purchases were made, but dividend stamps were issued instead. The few departments where the Society was not giving dividend under the former Climax system still did not issue stamps.

When the scheme was introduced, the basic dividend rate was five shillings and six pence (27½p), based on the value of the book surrendered for goods or as a share deposit plus bonus dividend of four shillings (20p) per book for members. Since that time, these terms were varied according to the amount of profit available for dividend. More dividend could accrue from the Dividend Stamp Scheme by way of special trade promotions on which extra stamps are given. This obviously increased the rate of the dividend. Stamps issued by any Society in the Scheme could be accepted by the RACS provided they were in an RACS stamp book, but not the certificates representing 1,200 stamps. Conversely, RACS stamps could go into other societies' books. This inter-changeability of Co-operative Stamps was not affected by other societies' different issue and redemption rates.

The stamp scheme operated in the Society in the following way. A stamp book was obtainable from any branch, and stamps were originally given on purchases at the rate of one for every six pence (2½p), but none for amounts less than this. After the introduction of the scheme the rates of stamp issue varied. When the book was full, it contained 1,200 stamps and was worth ten shillings (50p) and could be exchanged for the very wide range of goods, including food, in any of the Society's shops or stores or as a deposit on shares.

As an alternative, a book could be exchanged for cash at District Offices when the value was eight shillings (40p).

There was a distinct advantage in being a member because at the end of the year, members had their share accounts increased by a bonus dividend of four shillings (20p) for each book surrendered. A book would therefore be worth up to 14 shillings (70p) to a member as against 10 shillings (50p) for a non-member.

A statement showing share capital held, interest credited and the bonus dividend credited was sent to all members annually.

In the late 1970s and early 1980s, competition in the High Street became more intense, and the attraction of dividend stamps as a method of paying dividend as well as a trade promotional tool became less important. Consequently, it was decided to discontinue the issue of dividend stamps in Non-food and Pharmacy shops on 18th February 1985. Almost six years later, on 19th January 1991, stamps were discontinued in the Food division, Dairy division, and Fuel department.

APPENDIX 7
SOUTH SUBURBAN CO-OPERATIVE SOCIETY

SPONSORED GROUPS AND ACTIVITIES AT TIME OF MERGER

Member Relations/Education	Groups/Events
In-store Events	2
Candidates' Meetings	1

Member Organisations	
Co-operative Community Councils	5
CWG Branches	5
Miss Allen Essay Competition	1
SS Horticultual Society Shows	3
Beckenham Co-operative Mothers and Toddlers Group	1
Beckenham Co-operative Pre-School Playgroup	1
Beckenham Co-operative Ladies Keep Fit	1
Beckenham Co-operative Young Wives	1
Croydon Male Voice Choir	15
Croydon Co-operative Band	11
Croydon Co-operative Budo Centre	1
Croydon Banjo, Mandolin, & Guitar Band	17

Staplehurst Marching Band   1

Work with Schools/Youth Groups

Woodcraft Folk:

    Elfins   10

    Pioneers   10

    Venturers   3

    Junior Arts Festival   1

    Arts Project for Schools   1

Staff Education

Staff Weekend   1

International Co-operative Day

Fairfield Halls Concert   1

South Norwood Recreation Ground Fete   1

BIBLIOGRAPHY

Attfield, John, *With Light of Knowledge,*
A Hundred Years of Education in the RACS. 1981.

Brown, W H, *A Century of London Co-operation.*

Brown, W H, *Co-operation in Kent.*

Bruce, Maurice, *The Coming of the Welfare State.*

Co-operative Union, *Congress Attendance Record*

Co-operative Union, *Congress Representation.* 1832.

Co-operative Union, *Reports to Congress.* 1890 - 1919.

Co-operative Union, *Handbook to Woolwich Co-operative Congress.* 1896.

CWS, *Home Magazine.* 1962 - 1964.

CWS, *Good Shopping.* 1965 - 1966.

Davis, W T and Neville, W B, *Jubilee History of the RACS.*

Joint Committee of London Co-operative Societies,
Amalgamation of the Metropolitan Societies, 1934.

Jones, Ben, *Co-operative Production.*

Loveridge, Basil, 'Education for Co-operators',
Journal of Co-operative Studies. January, 1998.

Message, Fred, FLA, 'The Woolwich RACS, 1868 - 1985',
Woolwich Antiquarian Society, 1988.

Neville, W B, *Co-operation in London,* 1936.

Neville, W B, *A Commentary on Amalgamation of the
Four Co-operative Societies in London.* 1937.

RACS, *Annual Reports to Members.* 1920 - 1984.

RACS, Education Department, *Report on Adult Education,* 1946 - 1947.

RACS, Education Department, *Comradeship*. 1897 - 1961.

RACS, *News of the RACS*.

RACS, *Press Cuttings Collection*, 1903 - 1939. (Unpublished).

RACS, *Quarterly Reports to Members*. 1953 - 1984.

RACS, *Together, Staff Magazine*, 1937 - 1984.

RACS, *The War Years*, 1939 - 1945.

Reeves, Joseph, *Sixty Years of Stupendous Progress*.

Reeves, Joseph, *A Century of Rochdale Co-operation*.

Registrar of Friendly Societies, *Annual Report*. 1871 - 1889; 1924.

Registrar of Friendly Societies, *Returns*.

Rhodes, Rita, *An Arsenal for Labour*. 1999.

Roffey, R A, *Looking Back, A Brief Historical Guide to the RACS Archives*.

SSCS, *Annual Reports*. 1946 - 1984.

Stewart, William, *Origins and History of the SSCS*, 1920 - 1947. (Unpublished).

INDEX